THE
LONG
HARD
ROAD

U.S. ARMY RANGER RICKY'S STORY
WITH REFLECTIONS

Ricky Lamar and Others

Sponsored by:
Veterans Twofish Foundation
P.O. Box 220
Brighton, CO 80601
www.veteranstwofish.org

Printed in the United States of America
ISBN: 978-1477583-60-9

First Printing: June 2012
Second Printing: December, 2012

Produced by Adora Productions

1. Veterans Issues
2. Grief and loss
3. Child Sexual Abuse
4. Autobiography
5. Reflections

DEDICATION

I dedicate this book to the fallen soldiers and the innocent children lost everyday. "*If God is for you, who can be against you.*" *(Romans 8:31)*

ACKNOWLEDGMENTS

Our gratitude to all of the people who contributed their story to this book, and the following generous people who donated their time and gifts to make this reflection possible: Drawings: Robert Martinez, Adam Steven Torres, and Scott Martinez. Editors: Don Burough, Cody Bushman, Ashley Burnet, Sara Burns, Heather Campbell, Kathleen Cooper, Jodie Dallas, Rita Finney, Kenneth Francis, Robert Garcia, Gary Glasenapp, Pamela Hertzog, Amanda Gonzales, Walter Hwozdyk, Ashley Leonard, Michelle Lopez, Cathy Oasheim, Toni Parsons, Tasheena Polanco, Tina Roberts, Lupe Rubio, Jo Ann Sanchez, Kevin Sullivan, Juanita Tamayo, Shannon White, Vivian White, and Nick Wozny. Thank you all for your hard work, support and encouragement. Most of all thanks to Chaplain McDonald who helped to bring me back to Christ.

FOREWORD

In 2010, after I started working on my book, *Twisted Logic, The Shadow of Suicide*, God asked me to reach out to veterans by providing free inspirational materials to them. At first, I resisted. I was already involved in producing inmates books and DVDs called "Maximum Saints" and was distributing them free to prisons and homeless shelters through Transformation Project Prison Ministry.

I didn't feel I had time to expand my ministry, but I heard about the high suicide rates among veterans and I realized God was trying to reach out to them. I shared with Reverend Bill Gamble, a retired veteran and pastor from People's United Methodist Church in Colorado Springs, what God had told me. I asked if his church could sponsor a veterans' project.

Without hesitation, he said, "Yes." Since then, his congregation has been distributing my books, DVDs, and audio books to veterans through military chaplains. To make this project grow, the Veterans Twofish Foundation, a 501(c)(3) non-profit corporation was started in 2011 with Reverend Gamble.

I had no idea how God was going to lead me with the veterans project. Then the Lord asked me to gather stories of veterans for a book to help the veterans. This was similar to what I had been doing with the prisoner's book project. Right after this project began, I met Ricky at Adams County Detention Facility (ACDF) where I work as a chaplain. When I learned that Ricky was a veteran, I asked him if he would like to write a story for a veterans' book.

Ricky has written one of the most profound and touching stories I have ever read. Through his story, God opened my heart to understand the hurts and pains of veterans, which I was ignorant about.

The Lord led me to share Ricky's story in the Chaplain's worship services. The reaction to Ricky's story has been phenomenal, I've never seen anything like it. People who were reading his story were weeping and many who were listening were crying. Several shared how much this story touched them. It is so awesome to see how God is using his story of pain, tears, and hurts to open people's hearts and bring healing.

It was a privilege and an honor to meet Ricky at ACDF. If God hadn't asked me to work on a veterans' book, I probably would never have asked him to write, so I give glory and honor to Jesus. Ricky's story helped me to understand why God asked me to reach out to veterans. May God bless you as you read this book as He has done with me.

Chaplain Yong Hui V. McDonald
Adams County Detention Facility
Brighton, Colorado

INTRODUCTION

Have you ever been to church and felt like the preacher couldn't relate? Ever read a Mary K. Baxter book and not felt like she'd ever been where you are? Maybe the televangelist doesn't seem right, just seems too perfect for you? Well, that ain't me.

My name is Ricky and I am in jail in Colorado. I am 27 and a drug dealer to some, a gangbanger to others. I have tattoos on my neck, arms, chest and legs. I fought as a Ranger in Afghanistan and have killed plenty.

In the past few years, I have lost what seems like everything. Since my 21st birthday, such a short time ago, my daughter was killed by one of my drug addict customers, while I was in jail. I have attempted suicide many times and failed. I decided to write this book for the imperfect ones that don't wear suits and ties, but still have a belief in God, in Jesus and in the Holy Spirit.

I am a real person and this is a true story. This is me talking to you, no one else; one believer to another, trying to work it all out and save my soul. This is a book that is guided by what God puts in my mind. So if I upset you, I am sorry in advance. I am from a dirty, white-trash trailer park in southwest Georgia, on the Florida-Georgia-Alabama line. I am still a poor country boy who was trying to make it in a big city world and was doing it the wrong way.

I have decided to give up "the game," drug dealing, gun shooting and making money. This is me saving my soul. So read with an open heart, because the Holy Spirit is guiding my hand as I write these reflections.

Ricky Lamar

CONTENTS

PART TWO - REFLECTIONS ON THE LONG HARD ROAD

APPENDICES

Romans 8:31-39
An Invitation
About The Authors

Resources:
GriefPathway Ventures LLC
Veterans Twofish Foundation
U.S. Department of Veterans Affairs (VA)
Transformation Project Prison Ministry

ILLUSTRATIONS

PART ONE:

THE LONG

HARD ROAD

1. The Pain

When I was 5, I learned a lot about grief and pain. The head teacher of my preschool, Joe Garey, started molesting my brother and me. If I go back, I guess that's when my pain all began. I wish there were clocks that let you rewind time so you could restart life, but there aren't. Life is not a game, you get what is thrown your way.

My mother was 16 years old when my older sister was born. My parents weren't meant to be young parents. They were meant to have fun first. They never had a chance to be kids. My sister, Olivia, was 3 when my twin brother, J, and I were born. We were all too needy. My sister did the best that she could. She got out of the chaos early. She met a good man and married him. I guess I am still angry at her for leaving us.

First off, so you know, this story of my life is not something to give me an excuse to be a bad kid, it is just my story. I am from the country, where beatings are considered whippings. The whole "spare-the-rod, spoil-the-child" idea was the motto for handling discipline.

I was in the pea patches, picking bushels of peas by the time I was seven years old. The best man I ever knew was my Gagga. Yes, I said, "Gagga." Kinda a strange word for most, but pretty much, my Mom's Dad. The second best man I ever knew was my Papa, my Dad's Dad. Those two taught me about work and life.

One of the two, my Gagga, taught me to farm and cut down trees. He passed away from cancer.

My Papa taught me how to work on cars and how to handle scrap metal, do body work, and build houses. He died of emphysema. Both of them died when I was 12.

I had another mentor, my uncle Sambo. He was the biggest dope dealer in the Tri-State area. I learned to sell dope at 13. I walked up to my uncle, Sambo, and simply said, "I wanna do what you do. I am tired of being hungry." He asked where my brother was. I told him that he was playing ball. My uncle told me that I would need my brother's help. He called my mother and asked if my brother and I could spend the summer with him.

We spent the entire summer floating up and down the Flint and Chattahoochee Rivers making all different kinds of Meth. He gave us each $10,000 cash and a pound of crank. He then taught us how to build up clients.

That's how I learned the dope game. I ended up with connects for coke, crack, pills and more. You name it, I could get it. I stole cars for fun and had guns that could rip through vests, all before I was 17. I was destroying a city, a whole region, before I was 18. All the while, I was still planning on playing football in college.

Sambo died when I was 26 from a gunshot wound to the back of the head. I look back now and think, "Did all that have to be going on?" I wish I could take it all back. Maybe everything would be different.

"Airborne"
by Robert Martinez

2. Star Football Players

By the time I turned 17, I had been a drug dealer for a long time. Trailer parks don't make for good lives, but I was also a star football player in southwest Georgia, where football is king. We even won state championships.

I was approached by every college you can think of and was planning, along with my twin brother, J, to go to Florida. To this day, I still love the Gators. Well, God planned otherwise.

My uncle, a law enforcement officer in southwest Georgia, noticed that my brother and I had been popping up with all kinds of outrageous things, clothes, jewelry, and cars. The Drug Enforcement Agency (DEA) had also been there. My uncle pulled us over and found a lot, and I mean a lot, of dope. He decided to give us a choice.

"I will report that I found all this, if you two will agree to join the Army," he offered. We had a choice . . . life in jail or fight for our freedom, literally. The devastation of 9/11 was on everyone's mind, so security was heightened.

We always thought we'd get out in four years, walk on at the University of Florida and still have a chance to play football. We were 2 of the top defensive backs in the nation and on ESPN's top 100 prospects.

We were going to go pro. All we had to do was to stay healthy. We decided if we were going to be in the Army, we would be Rangers, the very best the Army had to offer. We graduated from Ft. Benning together as Airborne Rangers.

3. Ranger School

Ranger School is pretty similar to the Navy's SEAL training, we're just tougher, LOL. I'm just kidding, don't get upset. In Ranger School, we started with 123 candidates and only 29 of us graduated.

It's 2:30 a.m., and we are doing cold weather training, which is learning to fight in the coldest weather in the world. All the gear in the world won't keep us warm. We just tried getting to sleep at 2:15. At 2:45 frags (loud grenades) are going off over our head, we are being yelled at, "Get in place! You're dead! You're dead."

Imagine being in -15° F. weather and having no communications with the outside world. You latch on to each other, and when the weak fall, you either get weaker or drive on.

Next is swamp training. They call us the snake eaters. We will kill and eat rattlers and water moccasins to survive. They taste like chicken, bad chicken.

Then mountain training, climbing up and down steep inclines, blisters on blisters. Learning to survive and fight in this, we learn everything.

Air assault training; the first rule is to make sure the rope is attached to a ground source, because they generate electricity. I watched a guy die from electrocution, roping out of a chopper.

The movie, Black Hawk Down, was mostly Rangers and Delta soldiers, which are strange breeds. I know a few even though "they don't exist."

Urban warfare is fighting and surviving in a city setting. It's not that fun, but it's the easiest. The ground is just harder, it's concrete. HALO School is high altitude, low opening parachute training.

Desert training and mountain training was the major focus because of the wars in Iraq and Afghanistan.

Our motto was either, "Mess with the best, die like the rest" or, "Rangers lead the way" depending on who you ask.

Pat Tillman, the ex NFL star, was a Ranger. I didn't know him and won't pretend like I did, but I bet Ranger School was just as much hell on him as it was on me.

We learned to cope with loss and grieving through the training in Ranger School. One thing we never did was leave one of our own behind. Rangers have a

"No man left behind" law, and they really stick to it. If you are dead, we take back your body. If you are captured, we come and get you. Rangers earn some medals that are presented to our widows and some that are never even seen by anyone. We even get imminent death pay. Imagine that, imminent death pay. They pay us extra, because more than likely, we were going to die.

4. Preacher

I met Preacher in Basic Training. After Basic, we went to Advanced Individual Training (AIT) and Jump (parachute training) School together. We met up again in R.I.P. (Ranger Indoctrination Program). Preacher told me about the Bible. He wasn't overbearing or anything - just letting us know that "the Bible says this" or "the Bible says that," and in Ranger school, you will listen to anything. It's hell.

Preacher, my brother, J, and another soldier by the name of Grop, and I were all inseparable. In the hottest months of the Georgia summer at Ranger school, Preacher preached and we listened, but only because of the stress we were all going through.

I never took God seriously until I was sent to Afghanistan. There were no "foxhole atheists," that's for sure. My R.I.P. instructors, hated the fact that we all stuck together and never broke, kind of like a strong rope.

From here, the rest gets interesting. We went to Ft. Bragg. Preacher, my brother J, Grop, 18 others and I were attached to a 12 man "Reaper Squad." The object of a Reaper Squad, is to kill quietly and efficiently. 1 shot, 1 kill, and sometimes we didn't even need our gun.

If you occupied a building and we entered it, your life was over. The "Black Ops" units in all branches of the Armed Forces all work together in some way, but I think that Ranger Reaper Squads are the best killers in the world. Ten of us against 200 insurgents are good odds and that is not an exaggeration.

While I was killing numerous people, I was also reading the Bible. It got me through the killings. I wasn't a Christian to begin with, but there was something that was about to happen that would eventually turn me into one.

5. Camp Hope

Twenty months into my deployment, a bullet tore into my throat and my leg from an AK-47. I felt I was dead. I looked at J, and I remember clear as day, saying, "I am dead, Bro."

He said, "Don't worry, Bro. I got you. Have faith." I remember asking God to take me home to my daughter, who was a toddler at the time. Preacher sewed my jugular and my neck shut in combat, not very easy. My brother carried my 250 pound body and my gear 5 miles to a medic chopper.

I woke up a week later in Camp Hope. I was alive. I had a feeling of purpose. I read the New Testament about this man, Jesus. Who is he? Why are we fighting the Muslims? Why are these kids being killed to save us? I started to believe the Bible. I kept my little camo New Testament with me everywhere and I talked to Preacher a lot. My brother did, too. If I believed it, there was a reason.

6. Black OPS

This is how a general operation by a Reaper Squad goes:

03:16 a.m.:
I have had no sleep, but I am wide awake. Intel says this hospital is a cover for Al Qaida activity, so here we go, all 18 of us. I am the point man (first to enter), my battle buddy and twin brother, J, is the second in line. We are in the hold of a stealth chopper. Intel says there could be anywhere from 30 to 100 Al Qaida members and sympathizers in the hospital. Some civilian causalities are expected. How many, we are not sure. We just know that they are all dead once we enter.

Preacher says a prayer, Blue cracks a dumb joke. We all laugh for no reason. My Flack jacket is hot. I want to be in America with my little girl, so I kiss her picture.

Preacher says, "If I don't make it, I'll see you when you get there." My K-pot is heavy with sweat and so is the rest of me. Bumpy, our pilot, flies the bird ever closer.

10 minutes out:
We go quiet. My weapon of choice; M16A4 assault rifle, triple clip, extended infra-red scope, and beam auto-dim night vision goggles.

5 minutes out:
J says, "I got you." I say, "I got you."

2 minutes out:
Almost there.

1 minute 10 seconds out: I am hooked up to rappel, .45 semi-auto pointed out, sliding onto the roof. Two teams are going out the other side to the ground. They enter the hospital from the main entrance. There will be no escape. My brother and I, and three other teams are on the roof, silent. Preacher is talking to Jesus, you can tell.

The first ground team says that they are in. We are live, it's go time. I enter the roof hatch and everyone follows. The "ten of hearts" (Code name for the insurgent that is the mission objective) is in here, we know it. My brother kicks the door in and I enter and yell clear.

I heard screams and cries, gun shots and concussion grenades. A man sends three shots into my Flak jacket, it's like a baseball bat to the chest, I am winded. J grabs me, we head to the chopper. He has picture proof that the ten of hearts is dead. The building is clear, we meet on the roof. We only have one injured, except when we count, we are missing one person. It is Preacher. How is this possible? With the chopper waiting, we clear the rooms one more time. Gunners are fighting off insurgents heading toward the hospital.

We can't leave. Kill everything and let God sort them out. Three hours later, Preacher is still missing. His battle buddy, Blue, won't stop searching. We did everything correctly and by the book. He is supposed to be here, but he is not. The Colonel calls in, saying that Al Qaida claims to have captured an Army Ranger. We are stunned.

We searched for Preacher. Three months later, we found his body in Kandahar, no head, his body was decayed. He had a cross tattoo on his chest, and that's how we knew it was him. We were still in shock.

I was struggling with faith, asking, "Why would this happen to someone as purely good as he was?" He had three kids and a wife, but he always said, "If I go, I will see you when you get there." I talked with others about God here and there, but not like I did with him.

This is the only OP that I will mention. It was the worst one I went on, losing a great friend and spiritual confidant was hard, and still is. Take a moment and imagine being Preacher, alone and tortured for his last three months before he was killed.

7. The Last Message

A month later I got captured as a POW in Afghanistan. You think jails here are bad? Try no food and torture; in real life. You only see it in movies.

While I was in a cave, captured, I found Romans 8:31-39 carved into the wall. The whole Scripture was there. I knew this was the Preacher's work, because this Scripture was his favorite one. It was the first Bible verse I learned from him. It was truly Preacher's last message to me. Go ahead read it. I could quote it but it wouldn't be the same. (If you don't have a Bible, it's on Page 122 in the Appendices)

8. My Brother

Four months later, I was rescued. My rescue is unbelievable, but I will tell you anyway. My brother threw a dart at the map and said, "Let's go get my brother."

Baby Boy Blue, Garrett and I were the only ones left. On the way out, I took one in the chest and it hit my back bone. At some point, we hit a roadside bomb that flipped the Humvee, and I cracked my skull. I remembered football; it was all I could do to survive the surgeries. My brother, J, didn't. He was brought to a medical unit without a heartbeat.

My brother was me, just better. We are 6 foot 4", brown hair and eyes with funny looking ears. I had an intense love for him like no other. Sometimes it seems I just didn't deserve him for a brother. Loyalty and respect were the most important things to us -- and never giving up on anything we started. His passing hurt like losing half of me and his memory is with me through everything. The love we had for each other was an unbreakable bond.

I was in Frankfurt Medical Base in Germany and I heard how my brother came to rescue me. My brother was praying for days and reading his Bible. Jr., one of my buddies was there and he told me that he kept asking what J was doing and he'd say simply, "Asking God where my brother is." He studied the big map over and over and prayed. Finally one morning, the day I was rescued, he prayed at the map, walked to the dart board on the other side of the room, then he took out a dart, closed his eyes and threw it at the map. If you were there, you probably thought he was crazy, but not these guys. We all fought together.

J then went into the commanding officer's office and asked for a platoon and a chopper. "That's crazy," was what he was told. J then politely explained that he didn't care if they wanted him to go ahead or not. He said, "I am going to get my brother." He found 12 reapers and a Blackhawk and went ahead with a rescue mission. His faith got this rescue operation sanctioned, with no Intel or any support from his platoon.

"Good-Bye"
by Robert Martinez

9. Captain Legs

All I had was my brother and my daughter that I had only
seen once. He was gone. Losing an identical twin is so
difficult. A part of you dies. Then for five months, I was
learning to walk again.

The chaplain at the hospital, Cpt. Dorscett, had no
legs but he always seemed joyful. I hated him. I hated life.
I wanted to die. I would throw away every Bible I was

given. I said, "To hell with the Bible; it's myths and tall tales." But I hated myself the most. My brother protected me. He had come for me and I couldn't protect him. It ate me up inside like cancer or some virus. It took me a month to be able to eat.

While I was being tortured in captivity, the Bible verses were going through my head. But after I was free, all I said was, "No God that loved me would do this." Even now, I sometimes think that, but it's a test of my faith. My girlfriend, the mother of my daughter, ran off with another man while I was gone. That was even worse, I guess.

The chaplain I spoke of, Captain Legs, I liked to call him, came one day and said, "You've got legs. Why not use them? Are you so weak minded that this will ruin you?"

I said, "I'm not strong enough."

We got into a yelling match. Nurses came and he told them to leave.

I said, "I've got nothing. I can't sleep. I barely eat. My brother is gone. I can't walk. If I had died, I'd be a hero. Now, I am nothing. She took my money. When I go home, I am homeless, so leave me alone."

And for the first time in over a month, I was sitting up. He said, "Well, someone cares," and threw the Bible on my bed. I had never read all of it, just the little ones we got overseas.

Everyday he said, "If your brother and Preacher didn't believe in you, you wouldn't be here." He walked me through the Bible day by day while I started getting back to a full man as I called it. I figured I'll never be 260 pounds, all muscle again. I was down to 125 pounds, laying there like a vegetable.

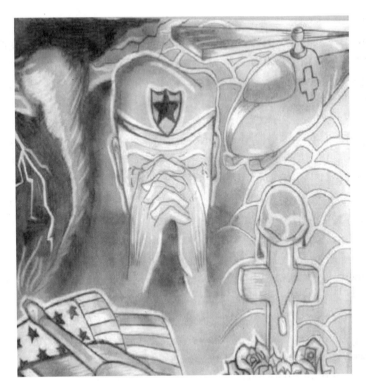

"A Ranger Cries"
by Robert Martinez

10. The Back Seat Driver

The finest story of faith in the Bible is the story of Job.
I realized there was always a chance of a future if I just
believed and tried. I have never been as faithful as Job,
ever. I guess I've always been what the Preacher called
a backseat driver Christian.

What that means is while there is no traffic and
things are smooth, I am okay to let Jesus drive; but when

it gets hard, I want to take the wheel and drive; even though I don't know the path, He does.

I feel like I can find a better way to get us there. Then I end up in a wreck like the Adams County Jail, looking at forever? Sound familiar? It's how people are. We can't just let God get us through. No. We've got to get through it and figure it out on our own. That doesn't work. I tried, trust me. Just look at your life and see. Go ahead. I will wait. How's it looking?

11. A Dream

When I got home from the military, in 2005, there were no jobs, anywhere, at all. I forgot the Bible and did what I knew to do; Sudafed, hydris, and lithium strips. Sixty-three days after the *Expiration, Term of Service* or "ETS" of my release from the Army, I set up a blockbuster drug deal.

I got in touch with some old connects. They said they needed 100 pounds. With my need for money, I stole supplies and got to work. I floated up and down the Chattahoochee River for over a month cooking crank.

I got it done and set up the deal. $10,000 a pound was a real good price. Do the math. That's one million dollars for me. That was my future, made in a month. Would I have quit? I don't know, but I was hyped with all these plans of what I would do with that much cash. I could get anything started for that.

I hated the Army, so when people said, "Go to the V.A, go to the V.A.," I didn't listen. I said, "That's for weaklings that can't make it. I got it."

I was seeing my baby girl, Robin, once a week, and I thought I had it made. I was selling smaller amounts of dope to get by, smoking weed and stuff; but I wasn't happy. Just trying to get paid a million was all that was on my mind. Ten grand here or there didn't matter. A million dollars could get me a life. When I had a 100 pounds of meth, I set up the deal. For some reason, I wasn't worried. Even though I hadn't seen these guys in years, I figured they were good. I would have fronted some of the cash if I had to.

On February 8, 2006, at about 1:30 a.m., I met with my old dope buddies, 100 pounds for a million cash. Sounds like I was dreaming the truest story ever told. We arranged to meet at the trailer park in Riverdale, Georgia. When I got there, I knew there was something wrong. The lights were out in the park and you know that gut feeling? Well, I had it.

When they got there, we talked a minute. Then they were like "So what's good, you got it or what?"

I said, "You know. I ain't out here for my health," so I got the bag out of my truck. Then I turned around to be looking down the barrel of a 9 millimeter. Thoughts raced through my mind and I wanted to get out of this.

Little J said, "Sorry dog, but that's a lot of cash, you got there."

I said, "Bro, you do realize that if you don't remove that pistol from my face, I'm gonna take it and kill all of you, right?" He laughed, and I didn't. I took his pistol and like a flash, three lives were gone. I was scared to death. "This is murder," I said. "What the hell now?"

Minutes later, the police pulled up and I was charged with a triple homicide, life without parole. My uncle bonded me out and luckily, I beat the murder charges. Little J's pistol was registered to him. I did 16 months for involuntary manslaughter because the dope was there, and that's the best deal I could get.

12. Hollywood

My military background got me sent to V.S.P. (Valdosta State Prison.) It's the worst prison in Georgia, high-max, violence all day. These Colorado jails are sweet in comparison. I didn't see my daughter until I was paroled. While I was there, I got back into the Bible.

My cell mate, Hollywood, was sentenced to life without parole. That means forever and ever, but he didn't hate God. He prayed every night and read his Bible.

He never talked to me about his faith until I asked him how he could believe in God. He asked me the strangest thing. "How can you not believe in God? Think of the air you breathe, the earth you walk on, and all the happiness you've ever felt. Where did it come from?"

I thought real hard and long and said, "Well, I don't know."

He said, "Well, I'll tell you. First read this front to back then get back with me."

He gave me a Bible. Another one. It seemed like everyone gave me a Bible. I spent 36 days reading it front to back. I got to know the Bible, the history of man and what true faith is. It's not seeing, it's believing no matter what. I wasn't sure either way, but I had a year to figure it out, so that's what I did.

I talked to Muslims, Christians, and Jews about the Bible and got all their opinions. It wasn't just one but all of them. I went to all the services offered and you know what? God was in the middle of it all.

During my time in Valdosta State, I fought almost everyday and was stabbed 16 times. Several times, I broke bones in my hands, ribs, and you name it. But that was a level 5 prison, that's how it was. At the end of the day, I stopped blaming God, my family and everyone else. I got down to the truth: I made the choices. I made the mistakes. No one else made me. Lots of trailer park and project kids are successful; so to all of you, look at yourself.

No one else did this to you. To all of you that say, "I didn't do it," listen. You put yourself in that position 99.9% of the time. So stop passing the blame, or stop reading now. This is for real people who want a real chance.

13. Struggles

Before love can come to you, you have to love yourself. I learned that in the war zone called V.S.P. I eventually got saved and baptized, ready for the world, so I thought. I got out of jail with no money, no home, nothing; and I tried to do it right. I saw my daughter a lot. I never went to church, but I believed.

Unable to care for myself, I found out I was having another child with a woman I truly loved, Ashleigh. While she was pregnant, I started hustling again. When my son was born on July 13, 2007, I was doing 3 months for violation of probation. That became my story: in and out of jail. I loved my kids and they loved me, but love didn't buy diapers and clothes. I was always selling dope. When I did 3 or 4 months in county jail, I told those I called jail house Christians, "Don't bring that crap around me." My favorite thing to say was, "If Jesus wasn't helping me out there, he sure ain't gonna help me in here."

I was a drug dealer and banger reppin' Grove Street in the trailer parks of Hometown, Gerogia, like I was 16 again. Shootouts and murders were normal, like everyday.

This is my struggle with my faith in God. Even right now, I'm in Adams County Detention Facility struggling to have faith. It's daily; I never get to the point that my faith is just there. Faith is a relationship you have to work at like any other. There came a point after the Army that I lost all my faith.

In June of 2010, I decided that I could no longer do probation and I was tired. I turned myself in and traded 24 months on paper for 5 months county time, a good trade in my book. I went and became a trustee. I was set to get out in November, right before Thanksgiving. I know this story is long, but imagine writing it on scrap paper with a two- inch golf pencil.

14. My Daughter

The worst thing happened to me while I was in jail. I'll do the best I can to be exact, but a lot of it is a blur. First off, I decided to be done with drugs all the way when I got out. I read the Bible and even joined prayer circles.

I had no violent charges. My manslaughter charges were sealed under the first offender act in Georgia. I wanted to get out and start a career in anything. I thought my faith was strong and that nothing could break it. Like Job, I was tested again, but unlike him, I failed. On October 3, 2010, Federal Marshals came to the jail. I was told to pack up. They transported me to the Sheriff's Department in another state. This is where my 7 year old daughter, Robin, lived with her mom and her mom's drug-addict, drug-dealing boyfriend, Jerry. I didn't like him and neither did Robin. Hell, my dog didn't even like him.

I have always lived by the saying kids and dogs like everybody that ain't bad and it's true. When I got there, Robin's mom was there. She, the deputies, and investigators informed me that Jerry was missing with Robin.

I was in shock. I couldn't swallow, my heart was caving in. "What do you mean, missing three days?" I had to be restrained from her mom. I was flipping out on her for leaving my baby alone with some man. She was obviously strung out on dope and I wanted to hurt her. But after calming down, I decided that all I wanted was to find my daughter. Then I would deal with that bastard and her mama.

We searched for what seemed like forever, put out an Amber alert, and did everything else. I couldn't sleep or eat or breathe or anything. I prayed day in and day out. I was crying, begging God for His help.

On October 8, 2010, the detectives told me they found a trailer on a nearby island. Neighbors thought Jerry had been in and out of it. His uncle was the owner. They saw Jerry leaving in his truck.

By the time we got there, the police were putting Jerry in their car. The detective in charge tried to stop me from going into the trailer. He said, "It would be easier if you didn't." I don't know why, but he let me go.

I remember the smell of copper and urine. The coppery smell was blood. The C.S.I.'s were putting the pieces of my little girl into a black bag. I saw her bloody face, eyes open, and I lost it.

The cops had to mace and taze me for busting the windows out of the cop car and pulling Jerry out. I was so hurt, not mad, but so hurt. I can't express it right now. It's worse than any torture you could put me through.

I read the confession Jerry gave. The things he described doing to my baby were unthinkable. He talked of how he raped her - just things the human mind can't wrap itself around without being sick. How he laughed in the interview makes my skin crawl even to this day.

Over a year has passed, and I still haven't seen her mom. The funeral was a blur. I heard that my daughter's mom killed herself and I believe it. I know it's wrong to blame her, but I did. I have, in this past year, held more hatred than ever before in my life: hatred for Jerry, hatred for Robin's mom, and most of all, hatred for God. How can a God that is supposed to love me, let my little girl be treated like that?

15. A Death Wish

How do I explain what it's been like this year? No God, believe me, no God—just hate, anger, and pain. I got high all the time. Things the average person would be scared of, I did. I lived with a death wish, not caring about life. Life's kind of weird, if you think about it. You think you're going one way, then all of a sudden, everything changes.

On September 14, at 2:00 a.m., when we pulled out of a McDonald's parking lot, a Task Force surrounded us. I knew we were in trouble. I could do nothing but laugh. It seemed like it was a set up, but it wasn't. Our headlights weren't on, so the police pulled us over. It seems funny now, but I truly believe that arrest saved my life.

While here in Adams County, I met Chaplain McDonald. After I read several of her books, I told her about my nightmares and that I was hearing voices: my daughter's cries asking why I couldn't be there, my brother saying he saved me and I should have saved him, and most of all, the memories.

I've learned that there are things you don't have any control over. Once you've seen them, you never forget. They have you and the devil uses these thoughts like a carpenter uses a hammer, as a tool to turn you away from Christ. This story has not been easy to write. I've thrown away 60 or so pages. I've edited and scribbled and rewritten things.

16. Courage

While I was reading a book by Tim Scott, God gave me this reflection. In the confused moment of death, we find ourselves alone with only what little sense we have of who we are and our love for others to guide us. We can all ask if we really know ourselves. Sometimes, it is hard to find an answer amidst the clutter of our lives.

In jail, I found an answer by taking away who I thought I was, putting everything I cherished on the line, and letting go of all the hatred I had and somehow holding things together and coming through it all. Maybe that's why I've decided to change.

In my life, I've found heroes are not born in the moment of victory. They are born, like J and the Preacher, in the lonely hour when everyone has abandoned them, when there is only dying hope, when they must stand against the rising tide of defeat. In that moment, there is surely doubt, but they fight on anyway because something lives deep in their souls. They trust in a belief they cannot see, touch, or explain.

While the faithless would flee, filled with fear, that voice inside that drives us can't be heard; those who believe stand firm because this is what God wants us to learn and tell our children, "Listen to yourself and trust what you hear. Faith, hope and love will lead you if you let them."

We are shaped by life experiences, and while the weak will crumble like the ungodly, that doesn't mean you have to. Keep trying. Humble yourself to the will of God. Make yourself available to God, and if you do die, know that your greatest gift will come after death.

Courage doesn't mean not being scared; we all are scared. Courage is doing what scares you the most. For me, it's leaving jail and not going to the $20,000 or $30,000 a month lifestyle.

It's starting from nothing and no longer poisoning people. It's the question of whether to keep going or fall to the side. Remember if you break down, if you give up and you die, you never have a chance to make up for it.

The road may be long and hard, but at the end, the blessings are worth more. This is my story, so from GA Boy: If God is for you, who could be against you? Never give up. Just keep trying. May God bless you for reading my story.

17. A Letter

To my brother J,

Well, how do I do this? I guess I just tell you how I feel. It seems like yesterday we were on our way to college, Go Gators! J, you know this letter is supposed to let you go, so I will try. I miss you Bro. I miss you so much. I am so sorry for not saving you. I'm the reason you are gone. It hurts, J, it hurts. There were so many times I needed you, and I've failed at everything without you. I've been to prison and jails repeatedly, and my little girl, your niece, well, you know.

How can I just stop hurting? I can't make the pain go away. All I have is a folded flag and some worthless medals. The picture that you, Preacher, Smoke, Blue, and I took when we got our Ranger tabs is worn out. Mom and Dad are finally trying to be parents. It took a long time, but, hey, better late than never.

I named my son after you. All this is just putting it off. Look, I love you, and I am sorry I couldn't save you like you did me. People always said I was a leader, but without you, I am nothing. I've turned my life over to God, so I will see you when I get there. Hold my baby like she is yours until I get there, like you always did. I want you to stop blaming me if you do, so I can sleep without these memories.

Please J, I just need to let you go. I'm sorry. I can't hold on to you anymore, so please help me to live without pain. I love you, but I just need to live without hurt. This is not goodbye, just I will see you when I get there.

Rangers lead the way, Hoooha!

Bubba

18. Reflections of a Lost Soul

I want to talk a little bit about child molestation. The man who molested me and my brother was a preschool superintendent named Joe Garey. That's when my pain all began. I won't sit here and say I forgive him. I lived with that, still do, and always will.

I told my parents, and I remember my Mama freaking out. We watched some video telling us to tell adults we trusted, if this ever happened to us. We were ashamed, but we still told our parents.

I guess the authorities in the late 80's didn't know how to deal with boys being molested; they investigated and charges were filed but didn't go far. After us, several more came forward, and later, pictures were found on the Internet. The sickest thing in the world is molestation. To this day, I refuse to watch a movie with anything close to molestation in it. Writing this is the first time I have ever wondered how long my daughter lived with it. I don't know if I will ever forgive Jerry or Joe Garey. I pray sometimes

for God to allow me to be the wrath, but the Bible says
that only God can judge. But how do you forgive
something like that? No one will ever be able to tell me
that being molested starts a cycle. I've never looked at a
child like that. I know what living with it is like: the
memories, the anger, the problems, dealing with authority
figures. I lashed out at others, and guess I still do
because the pain festers inside your soul. Right now I am
trying to get past it, but it won't be easy. It will be a long
road.

Anyone that uses being molested as an excuse to
do the same, I laugh at. Why would you touch another
child after growing up with it? I am coming to terms, as I
write this, that maybe my daughter was molested for
years without me knowing. It hurts so bad, that I am
crying trying to finish this.

All I can say is, may God have mercy if I cannot find
forgiveness. If I can, it is truly a miracle from Jesus
himself, but through Him, I am finally trying.

19. Shattered Dream

It's so hard to have resentment, sadness, and anger
bottled up. That's not an excuse, but it is the reason I've
lashed out and caught five felonies. They are all small
financial crimes.

You see, it's not just my past life. When you watch
those T.V. documentary dramas showing coming home
from war, you get the guy who never saw real live infantry
combat, not like the Rangers, Green Berets, Force
Recon, Combat Controllers, SEALS, Scouts, Cav, and

Reaper Squads. Most of these guys DD214s (Discharge papers) all look like mine. "He came in, then left from this base for some off-the-wall medical reason." All the while, you are still fighting.

The shows on T.V. show truck drivers or 12 month tour guys who are coming home to waiting wives and kids, coming home to a perfect family life. What about the injured who feel worthless? What about the ones who have no job to return to? No family to meet them? No wife because she left him? What about the guy who isn't getting paid anymore, has no idea where he is going to go, the guy who is just tired of killing? Well, Ricky is that guy.

I had nothing to come back to, but I couldn't focus on it. I just tried to be normal. I tried so hard, but it didn't work. I started dreaming of suicide. I cut myself just to feel the pain. Life meant nothing to me. I think they should do a T.V. special on people like that: the ones who have nightmares so bad they are scared to sleep; the ones who are getting high to stop the pain.

I heard somewhere that as much as seventy percent of the prisoners in the U. S. are ex-military in some states. I also heard that seventy percent of the homeless people are ex-military.

The military is structured, it is outlined in chalk. All that civilians see are uniforms and salutes. Let's dig deeper and take a look at the five percent that have attempted suicide after coming back from these two wars over the past ten years. It's a huge number. Just for the record, I'm not ranting; I'm telling you my story.

Many like me live through this same pain. We need an entry program back into civilian life, long term psychological care and all kinds of other support that just isn't available.

Life isn't sugar coated like it is on T.V. It took all of my struggles to get me where I am now. I read my Bible, I talk to God. For a long time, He didn't talk back, but now I realize I just wasn't listening.

I am addicted to the fast life, drugs, money, women, and cars. But thanks to the grace of God, I am changing. Chaplain McDonald and her books have gotten me to read the Bible again.

Now, I rely on Jesus for my strength, Him and no one else. I am doing things I never would have done before.

20. Battle Buddies

Out of my original Reaper Squad in Afghanistan, I am the last survivor. The camaraderie between Rangers is like no other. Once a Ranger, you are always my brother.

I believe that felons should be accepted in the military. We've got more reason to fight, and being in jail and prison prepares you for life without anyone but your brothers to have your back. I thought I was tough, but life has made me tougher.

If I could re-enlist today, I would, just for the structure and stability that comes with Army life. My biggest wish is to be back in the Army right now, with my fellow Rangers consoling me about my daughter. It is an unbreakable bond, so lead the way, all you fellow Rangers, get out of wherever you are and lead others to God. Hoooah!

For all of my soldiers: We've got to be there for each other, we've got to pray and lead our brothers. Let's do it like "Battle Buddies," so the next generation isn't lost like so many of us.

21. Letting Go

Shortly after starting this writing project, the judge gave me a bond. For some reason, I didn't call my dope buddies to bail me out, even though they would have. I didn't call them, and I am still here three and a half months later.

I have been getting right with God. If God wants me out, I will get out on December 22. If He doesn't want me out, I won't leave. I am just letting go and letting God handle it. All of it, not some of it, and I am not taking it back.

I think Preacher, J, and my daughter deserve heaven, and for my sin, my payment is here on earth, in this spiritual battle ground. I hope they are watching me, because I am finally getting through the pain and loving God. Even in jail, I am happy. Life is good with God, and there are no gunshots. May all be blessed.

22. The Answers

"My dear Lord Jesus, how is it that you can find favor in someone as unworthy as me?" I asked while walking with my Savior one day. I tried so hard to get an answer for many days, until one day after being put into the hole, and

THE ANSWERS / 41

then on suicide watch. I met a trustee and she helped me answer God's questions of why it had to be me. One day she was cleaning and read the ID on my door. When I came out for my one hour of day space time, this young girl, maybe only 21 or 22, asked me where I was from.

I replied, "Georgia."

She said, "Oh, my God! I read your story in the Chaplain's Worship Service."

She told me about all of the people that wept. Not so much for me, but for their lives and the possibility of their children being molested. There were many other possible reasons, but it touched me.

Then I thought, or more like Jesus and the Holy Spirit said, "You have been through so much, you can relate to others' pain. Without pain, there cannot be love, and without sadness, how can you appreciate true happiness?" I guess that's true.

Others in jail talk to me because we come from the same bad places. When I see the young ones headed down the same path I took, that hurts me. Just for the record, I started writing for me to let my pain out, no other reason. Not to help Chaplain McDonald or any other person. I have no thoughts of fame or fortune. I just wanted to relieve some pain, and let go of some anger.

I am not perfect, as none of us can be, but I want to be better. I don't want to poison my communities anymore. I have been all over and sold pills, pot, and meth everywhere, but I am done with that, no matter what. I am still processing the grief from my life, but I guess it gets easier. Well, maybe if you unbottle it, it does. I have found that prayer and writing have made things easier for me. If you are in jail, walk, it clears the mind.

Never take something out on someone, if it is not their fault. I've fought many people, and I found it doesn't help.

I've been on suicide watch, it's terrible. The best help is Scripture, lots of Scripture. Or read the Maximum Saints books, they help too.

Stay away from drugs. They don't help anyone in or out of jail. It's not gonna help, so keep pushing through the pain. Like Josh Turner says, "If you're goin' through hell, keep on movin', you might get out before the devil even knows you're there." Why give up? I've given up, I've tried to kill myself. I have been everything that you have. I am 27 without a purchase on life. Just me and a nice outfit, that's it. So, where do I go from here? I am letting God lead me through life right now. Hopefully I can let that be enough, maybe if I pray it will be, maybe not. Right now, I am faithed up with all of the faith in the world.

23. A Vision

My daughter was 7 years old when she passed. She had long, curly brown hair and the prettiest hazel eyes. Her laugh could make you smile through anything. She was my angel. She used to call me and tell on her mom for making her mad. Nothing made me happier than hearing, "I love you, Daddy," or getting a kiss from her.

I'm lucky to have been able to be her dad, to hear her laugh, and to find her little Dora doll when she lost it. I should thank God for that, even though she's gone now, because at least I have her memory.

One night, while I was still in the hole, I had visions of my daughter and brother all day long. I am fighting against the urge to kill myself. All I think is, "I wish I could die." I look at the drawing representing my brother and daughter -- and break down again.

I can't read because the lines blur. My body is tense and restless. I beg God again, "Help me, please take this pain away." But the visions of my dead brother and brutalized daughter don't end. I hear the voices, as I have for days. I am going crazy.

The officer came by and asked, "Are you okay?" I kept praying and said, "Yes, I'll be fine." All of a sudden, I grabbed the drawing and cried my millionth tear.

I'd been in and out of the medical unit on suicide watch, but I refused to go back. Three more weeks of being in the hole -- and I will be able to cope more with life behind bars in the general population. I'm not friends with myself, so the hole gets to me a lot.

As I stared at the drawing, I prayed more and more, and again asked God for mercy. Then the picture changed to a serene, happy image of my daughter, brother, and best friend, Preacher, in Heaven. It's as realistic as a photograph.

Then my baby said, "Stop crying, Daddy."

And J said, "We're here forever."

Preacher said, "We ain't goin' nowhere. We'll see you when you get here."

I laughed, I told them I miss them all so much. "Hey, Rangers lead the way," J said, "Show the world how to be as good as you can be. Time is just time, but souls live forever."

Robin laughed and said, "Yeah, silly, I love you, Daddy." It felt like her little arms were hugging me. She told me bye, and the picture changed again, back into the original drawing. After this, my time in the hole got easier. Actually, everything did. If you see me, you can tell. I smile more, laugh more, and even behind bars, I enjoy life more.

These walls don't make us who we are. We are here, we've got to deal with it and we can't change it. So, why grieve about lost ones? They are much happier where they are. The world, in or out of jail, is temporary, so why concern ourselves with it?

All that I can say is the Holy Spirit has changed my perspective on everything. Not just about myself, but about the world. This occurred while doing a month and a half in the hole, believe it or not. Even if it was only a dream, it changed me, so let's thank the Father for our lives, not curse Him for the bad spots.

This picture has helped me so much. I see it as my brother and my daughter waiting for me in heaven.

"Waiting on You"
by Robert Martinez

24. Forgiveness

The question I am asked the most is, "If you could change one thing, what would it be?" My answer is, "Nothing, because good or bad, like it or not, it made me who I am and that's all I've got left, me."

Am I better than anyone? No, definitely not. I am not better. If anything, I am worse. I am still learning about God and how to be more like Jesus. But I wake up and get out of bed and try to smile.

I have had plenty of loss in my life, but who hasn't. I just put mine into words, maybe you didn't. I am not Shakespeare. I will never be a famous author, but maybe I can tell you how I got through all the pain.

First, I bottled it up. I refused to forgive. I swore I'd hate those who hurt me. We would be mortal enemies. That worked great. I started doing the drugs I was selling more and more. I started fighting random people. Hatred is truly a demon that festers when you hold back forgiveness. The person I hated the most -- guess who? After I got past God and this guy or that girl, the person I truly hated was myself!

I didn't know that I hated myself for years. Don't I feel dumb? I've found out that without love for yourself, you cannot love anyone else. First I had to grieve. I had to kinda bleed. That's what I am doing as I write, I'm bleeding. I'm squeezing the infection out of a sore. You see, life is like your body.

The person that said, "What doesn't kill you, makes you stronger," is an idiot. If you get shot, your body weakens. Believe me, I know. The only thing that gets stronger through time is your mind; just your mind and that only works if you overcome the breakdowns. I think crying is therapeutic, but only sometimes. I'm a grown man, a broken bone doesn't make me cry, but emotional pain does.

Have you ever been so hurt you couldn't cry? That's real pain. When you are in jail and a loved one dies, you can't spend one more minute with them. That's pain. You blame yourself, but you won't admit it. That's when hatred builds.

What is forgiveness? Is it forgetting? No! That forgive and forget motto is impossible. How do you forget what someone has done? You can't. You have to deal with it and get through the hate. That's forgiveness. I'm writing this book for those who need to deal with pain, so if you've never been hurt, sorry this is the wrong book for you. But if you are human, you have. Chances are if you are reading this, you are trying to find a way to live through the grief, the turmoil, and the pain.

Life isn't easy, but we are put here to serve God. My God is bigger than anything on earth; I'm still trying to get that through my skull. One way or the other, God's gonna win, whether I like it or not. I mess up a lot. I'm not perfect but my imperfections make me human, so now that you know I'm human, are you? Are you perfect? Since that's out of the way, I'm going to tell you how I deal with life.

I've gone from the bottom of the bottom, worst of the worst to being a decent person. It starts with this -- are you ready? Now, let's get started. The world is an ocean of pain and we are the fish living in this ocean.

The Bible tells us these are the end times and we need to prepare. To prepare we must forgive and to forgive, we must process grief. That's the only way to make it work, so step one of processing grief is to accept the pain. You have to allow yourself to hurt first. You've got to feel the raw pain that makes you break down.

I've broken down more in the past few months, since I started writing than ever before. The tears seem like they will never end. And your heart, well, it feels like it's being squeezed over and over by 10,000 pounds of pressure. I'm not saying this is easy or fun, but it has to happen. I'm not sure what pain you are feeling, but I've probably been there. I was molested. I lost a child to a brutal murder. My twin brother died beside me in combat. I've been where you are. Probably, everything you are considering, I have considered.

I think Eminem said, "Sometimes I cut myself to see how much it bleeds." It's like adrenaline. The pain is such a sudden rush for me. I've got hundreds of scars on my forearms, where I cut myself and I understand. It releases a little, but we both know it comes back. And every time, it will be back.

Punching walls is another tactic that never works because the walls don't punch back and you can't do much with broken hands. Option three is fighting. The problem with fighting is you are just uncapping the fury, letting a demon free for a little while, then going to jail so you can try to figure out what happened to your life again.

That's what I am doing now, figuring out and processing grief in jail, while I try to help someone else out, because God's got a purpose for me. We have things in common we've both lived through. There's too much for this to be just a fluke, that we're still living. Right?

To my soldiers, I know its hard coming home. Good God, it's hard. You are not the same as you were. Killing takes part of you, and even without the killing, the environment changes you. I've gone to war and prison and they both leave you empty. You feel like there is no emotion left. But if you open your Bible, read, and pray, after a while it helps.

It's not immediate, there is no quick-fix program. It takes time. And before you put that gun in your mouth, let me tell you that ain't it either. There are too many soldiers and prisoners killing themselves. It's like after seeing the worst, there is no hope.

But brothers and sisters, there is hope. Just call on Jesus. Beg Him and His Holy Spirit to lead you. You are homeless? So what, who cares! It could always be worse. Someone else is going through the same thing. As followers of Christ, we are not to fall by the wayside like the weak and worthless. We are to fall to our knees and beg for direction to lead the weak. You got life in prison? So what, thank God you haven't got any bills. You are crippled? Been there, done that. Now, I wish I didn't have to walk so much.

Praise Jesus for everyday, for the beauty of the clouds and for the mountains. When will we worthless humans stop going, "Oh it's so terrible, God, please, it's so bad, why God, why?" Well, let me tell you why, because you have to lead another, that's why. You don't need to ask God. The question has already been answered, to forgive or to lead another you must struggle. None of us have experienced the losses like Job did. Yet, are any of us as faithful? I'm not. I'm sure as hell not, but I'm trying. I won't give in to the devil and take my life because once you are gone, how many can you lead to Christ? How many souls can you save? Not one. That's zero and we can chalk-up all the ones you could've helped as a loss. Put that gun down so we can move on with this.

25. Faith

Are you hurting? Okay. I feel you. God doesn't listen? I feel you. My twin brother died saving me. I truly have felt that. You think it's all your fault? That's what I thought too. It's just God's plan. God's plan is perfect without fail and solid. You've got to have faith. F-A-I-T-H. The biggest five letter word ever. That's the faith we all need.

I was a POW and before I was rescued in Afghanistan, my buddy, Preacher, always said, "See you when you get there!" before every OP because he knew he was going to heaven without a doubt. Job through all his trials never lost faith. Now, I cannot say I'll always have faith, but I'll always try my best.

The best part about God is He doesn't expect perfection. If you do mess up and fall to the wayside, get on your knees and pray to God. He will forgive you. How do I know? The Bible says so. It says I will be forgiven if I ask and that's faith.

I was born into sin and I am a sinner. We all were; the rich and the poor. Even our presidents and priests are born to sin. You have to have faith in God's willingness to forgive. I know it's hard, but that's the beginning of everything. Faith, we all stumble. We all fall. Let's just all try to have faith. Once we have faith, it all gets easier.

26. Depressed

Have you ever been depressed? Not sad -- depressed.
I mean so depressed you get sick. You cannot get out of
bed. You can't eat anything. You are just sick. You want
to die. You wish everyone would leave you alone. I have.
I've cried till I threw up. My daughter was taken at such a
young age. Her spirit seemed to haunt me through
pictures, memories and everything.

The same thing happened when my brother J was
taken. It's all a test of faith. It doesn't seem fair, but we all
go through a lot. The rich and poor, everyone struggles
with pain. Some seem to struggle more than others.
When the time comes to face God, how we handled our
struggles, will be the measure of our faith. Faith is not a
science or test of perfection. My faith is there for a reason,
even if I sometimes cannot see it.

For me, I am sure I will be classified for all the
lapses. I've sworn I hated God, then begged for
forgiveness. I've given up my faith, then grabbed it back.
I've been back and forth with God my whole life.

Some days, I still hate life. Life is hard. Yet, after
everything, I still think God has a plan for all of us. Not just
me, all of us. The ones we lose are better off. Why cry for
them? When we cry for a loved one passing, we are really
crying for our loss, we are crying for ourselves. I know you
heard that before, but it's the truth I've learned.

I grew up in a trailer park that made most projects
seem like the suburbs. Fighting every day, I was stabbed
twice by the time I turned 13. I was selling dope and was
a banger. All the guys I knew are now dead or doing
major prison time so it's easy to just give up. I've been

doing time since leaving the Army -- always in and out. Maybe you have had to do that too. It gets old quick, doesn't it? It did for me, but I kept going back to it every time I got out.

The need for the fast life was stronger than anything else. I enjoyed the power to say, "Jump," and they jumped. That was my mask for depression all my life and how I dealt with it. I covered depression with drugs and money, not to mention anger.

To kill someone doesn't make you tough. I know killers, real killers. One guy I know just died in a robbery. God rest his soul. Bill was a good person, but the money drove him to do bad. Money covers troubled souls. I've smoked and drank with Bill. Now, he is in Heaven. All the trouble from the streets is gone, but at what cost? His whole family is crying. His sons are growing up in the same environment. Is that what you want? I don't. I've got to change - to get better and learn from my friends who have showed me how to unintentionally commit suicide.

If you die, who tells your kids about Jesus? Who teaches your children sports or protects them? The life you lead cannot mask pain forever. I've always seemed happy, but I'm happier writing books for God than any day I made $10,000. That was a mask for depression. This is a smile on paper that's coming through like a new tattoo, permanent.

Jesus is my answer to all, no matter how big or small. Give your problem to our Savior. He was crucified. If He can take that, these problems are nothing. Let Jesus deal with it. Read the Bible and just pray till your knees are broken, then pray some more. It won't come immediately, but through faith, He will heal your pain.

27. Drugs

Sleepless Nights

Hiding from the shadow people
The top of the world is amongst people
Alone I sit, days into this binge
I can't sleep, I can't eat
My body shuts down
As the bowl goes round and round
In my veins the poison goes
And out it goes with smoke I blow
I give it up once again
Until again the world will spin
The people I love, they don't know
At least I think that they don't know
My smile is not the same
As I stay awake, just one more day
One day at a time
I reclaim my peace of mind
I wish I could turn back the hands of time
But until then, I will load the bowl
One more time
And lose my pride, as I forget sleep
One more time.

For those who don't know, drugs are bad, real bad. And so are gangs. I remember back when I was about 16, selling meth and a lot of stories that would make you sick, stories of things addicts would do to get dope.

Most people know a few addicts, but I know a lot. So, to the young, before you start on the drugs, I will tell you a story of Linda. Linda started buying from me when she was 18 and I was 13. She was the prom queen and head cheerleader. She started community college. Her parents were very wealthy.

By the time she was 19, she had dropped out of college due to her drug problem. Linda hated to admit it, but even her family knew. And while they did take care of her and her bills, they were about to stop giving her cash.

I was slowly watching this girl destroy herself and I didn't care. I needed that money -- I thrived on it. I remember her offering sex, this beautiful woman, and I was only 13. At 19, she was selling herself to the 14 year old drug dealer for dope.

My whole crew made fun of her. We treated those addicted girls like nothing, because we had what they wanted. Now they make me sick, but back then drugs were all fun and games. I couldn't care less for the lives I destroyed.

Drugs take your pride and destroy what you were, making you a different person. I hate drugs. I've wasted millions on drugs and the life around drugs; jewelry, clothes, cars, and my so-called friends, you name it.

Whether you sell or do drugs, it's still gonna take parts of you away. You smile, but are never happy. You are never at ease, either the Drug Task Force or the Jack boys can come at any time. (Jack boys rob the drug dealers.) And the user just wants more. I sit here and wish I could take it back.

28. Description of Jail

Imagine everything you hold dear ripped away and then being given a set of clothes you will wear everyday. Five television channels, a small room, a desk, toilet and a sink. Now, imagine barely having enough food to feed your hunger. Then, ponder going to sleep with your stomach growling, wishing for the ability to choose what to eat.

Phone calls to home are ridiculously expensive and you realize that people are making money to keep you caged up. You get a thin blue mat to lay on while you try to figure how you got here. You are given the same terrible food everyday and on Christmas, Thanksgiving and other holidays you get sandwiches. You also have to be aware of every threat that is around you, because you may need to fight at any time. You watch other people leave and wish it was you.

Your girl forgets you, because when you are out of sight you are out of mind. Everyone's life moves on, while yours is never changing. You start to forget people's faces, even your kids. They grow up, walk, talk and start school but your life is unchanging. You have no privacy. You cry in the shower, if you are alone. You change your sheets and clothes once, maybe twice a week.

Does this sound fun? This treatment is for everyone in jail. This is how we discipline everyone, whether they are guilty or not, if they cannot make bail. This is how we are treated and some officers see inmates as less than human. This is jail.

It seems I should give some insight on how jail becomes a revolving door. First, you get arrested. The first time is the worst. It's the hardest to deal with. Once you are arrested, you are put in a cell and your life becomes repetitive. If you are wealthy, you could get out. You just pay a little money and you can usually bond out. But let's assume you are poor.

If you are poor, you can't afford to bond out, and you definitely can't afford a lawyer. You have a public defender who just wants you to take a plea bargain, guilty or not so your off his or her huge case load. Let's say you've got a drug charge and you get two years plus parole. You will always have probation or parole. After two years you're out of jail.

While you were in jail, you lost your job, car, home--everything. You have fines to pay so you have to have money. If you don't pay your fines, you go back to jail and you definitely don't want that. You are also homeless.

One of the rules of probation is you must have a stable job and home. But you are a felon. A lot of jobs don't hire felons; a lot of places don't rent to felons either. So you are stuck. What do you do? As bad as you don't want to, you call your old connect. He finds you some dope now. You sell that, but then you gotta keep that up to pay the bills, so you are back out there running the streets, selling dope, toting a gun, and making money as you sell more dope. You get deeper and deeper into the game, which is really not a game but a deadly life style that you cannot escape once you are immersed into it.

The biggest problem is the lack of a support system. I finally have one. It's a core group of people to help you when you get out. They help you find somewhere to live. Support people help you find a job. Of course there is no perfect way, but this is a start. Maybe if you could get a place to live until you get a job, you wouldn't go back to drugs so quickly. Or maybe if you had a church to help you with anything, your life might not end up in the toilet once again.

So, if you are in jail, find a support system. If it's your son, daughter or friend, help them get it figured out. Let's stop the repeats of the repeats. Jail is not the place for human beings and if we get together, we can stop the door from spinning around over and over again.

29. A Reflection On Jail

Today I feel like writing because my spirit is restless. I want out of jail so bad. But to do so means to go back to selling drugs. That just isn't a good idea. And even though I know the desire is still there, I miss freedom in this lonely cell and would give my life for one minute of true freedom.

Where would I be now if I was free? The answer seems to be unfathomable. I can't even begin to imagine life out of jail. I've been here six months and nothing is happening to move me closer to freedom. Some days, the walls collapse in on me and I can't bring myself to pray. And yes, I know this is part of jail. I have trouble dealing with it. I've done lots of time, yet all I want to do is cry so I can forget that I'm in here. Jail is no place for anyone. This is not the life for anyone.

Sometimes I miss war because it wasn't the same thing everyday. Jail is a repeat, over and over again. One day to the next there is no change and sometimes I fear I could be here forever. I am so tired of cages and this is the reflection of jail one day to the next. I can't describe the monotony and how one day becomes another in this terrible place so before you end up here, listen to this. This is the reflection of life in jail. In these unforgiving walls, it seems all is lost, even your soul.

30. Judgment

You're still reading, so that's good. This reflection is directed to both young and old, but it's going to start with the young. Don't give up on me until you make it through the whole thing. I promise the Holy Spirit is leading this, not me, it's just my hand and a pencil. I'm a recovering sinner. I was a drug dealer and a gang banger. My friends are all sinners, addicts, murderers, gang members and convicts. That or soldiers. No joke. No lies. We are so quick to condemn dealers and gang members. I know hardcore gang bangers, but those same people, if raised in suburban America would be in colleges.

Many of the drug dealers I know read their Bible and pray just like any Christian. Look at the prostitute and ask what would you do if your kids were crying, hungry, their dad was in jail, and you couldn't find a job.

Jesus came to this world to die for our sins, not to condemn the sinners. But we all judge the wino or crack head bum. We don't look in their eyes, but what if ten years ago, he had a wife and child and a drunk driver killed them both. How would you have handled that? I got high on my supply after I lost my baby.

I know perfect soldiers who are now heroin addicts, because they can't handle the memories. If you haven't been there, don't judge.

We get excited when our favorite sports team gets a great player. I know I do but how come we have millions living on a few hundred bucks or less a month, yet we're happy these special people get 100 million dollar contracts to play ball. We elect millionaires and billionaires into the presidency who have no mercy for the issues of poverty.

All I've ever wanted was to be comfortable and not have to struggle to eat. But when honest jobs don't come, that's when drug dealers, gang bangers, strippers, and hustlers choose their alternative lifestyles.

We have to make a change in this world. Not just America—the world. It can't be, "Well Jimmy ain't changing, so I won't either." It starts with one. Just one person. Judgment is for God. If you are not that wino or killer, you don't know why. I sold dope because it's all I truly knew how to do.

I went in the Army and killed people. The Army was supposed to change the way my life was going, stop the gangs and drugs. Truthfully, with no guidance, what is there to do, but to go for what you know and I know the streets. I can take a dollar and a month later have $20,000. By then it's like a solid business. People are relying on me to support their family, so I know how hard it is to quit. Could you let your family starve? I couldn't. That's why God is the only one who is allowed judgment. I'm not making excuses. I'm giving the dynamics. Why not stop judging and start helping? It's pretty easy.

While I was walking with the Lord today, it came to me, or better yet, He brought to my mind, humbleness. It is so hard for us to be humble. Some seem to do it easily. One person who comes to my mind, who has become a household name, is the Bronco Football Team Quarterback, Tim Tebow. Tim Tebow embodies humbleness. If you watch him, after his games, he always thanks Jesus first. I have trouble with that sometimes. Do you? Think about it. What does it mean to be humble? First, you must not be prideful by taking all the glory for yourself because that glory belongs to God.

How can we be prideful of the outcomes that we are not responsible for? We all are. But, hey, Jesus forgives. He forgives everything, if you ask. To humble yourself is to say "Lord, I give the glory to you and no one else." Think about that and what that means. It's hard to do, but I think we are all capable of bowing to the will of God.

The question is, will you let go and let God? It took 27 years for me to humble myself and it has been difficult. I had to act like a child who knows nothing, but finally I got it. I'm not perfect and we are not meant to be, but through God we can humble ourselves so that our judgment of each other is gone. We have to be humble and ask Jesus to help us when we are prideful. When we do the answers and God's power will come.

31. Change

I'm having trouble writing this. I'm trying to find some perspective. The rich judge the poor, and the poor judge the rich. That might be what really hampers the evolution of society. I grew up blaming the rich for all my troubles, like they could have stopped them.

I have known rich addicts who wouldn't have spoken to me if I wasn't the dope man. For the rich to judge the poor, or the poor to judge the rich, is like racism. It's hating based on how they look before you know them. I'm a white guy, but I grew up in a mixed area that was predominately black, so I've never understood that kind of racism. Some of the best friends I ever had were black. Baby Blue was a Ranger with me and was one of my closest friends.

However, I've recently discovered that I have an inner dislike for the wealthy. It's because I was taught that the rich keep the poor down. It could be true sometimes, but sometimes it's not. We as humans have to stop our judgment toward each other. Life is so precious and we waste it on hating. All of us have seen the bum outside the liquor store and felt like we were better than him.

Let's ask ourselves what made him that way? Why is he a drunk or drug addict? Do you think he really was born that way or someone like me woke up and said, "I wanna sell dope." For me, it was as if I didn't have a choice. I lacked values. I was never a church goer, nor were my parents.

I expected to grow up to be good in spite of it all. Some are able to do it, but how could I, when all that was around me were drugs and violence? The people I knew to be the top guys were all drug dealers and didn't have to work. They drove fancy cars, while I starved and my parents worked themselves to death. With no leadership, I fell to gangs.

My sister didn't. She is a teacher, married to the mayor's son with a decent life. She's never smoked or done drugs. Somehow we ended up different. How did she do it? I don't know. I was 12 and she was 16 when our two grandfathers died. Maybe she already had her life planned and me and J were still figuring life out. She grew up with my parents in drug and gang infested places and she didn't turn out like me. I know rich kids that end up just like me, so we can't judge. Drugs turned me into evil, pure evil. Gang banging is real and it's everywhere.

So tell me, why can't we stop it? Drugs kill, but we can't stop it. We have to help each other. Teach each other, or better yet, love each other. No one will change, if we all wait on someone else to change. A friend explained to me that's what we do, we wait on the world to change. Well, I'm not waiting. Help me, let's change the world.

32. Fight

I see you are still reading. That's impressive because I can't even believe I'm still writing. But, every day God tells me this has meaning. The world can be better. Here in America we are so caught up in all the stuff we think is bad. We don't know or we forget that there are worse places.

Even I'm guilty of that, so don't think I'm just saying "you," I say "we." We have church, someplace where people won't kill us for believing in Jesus. I've been in countries where you would be killed for a Bible being found on you. Places where you would never forget that America is free. Not perfect, but yes, free. Free to believe in any God you want.

My God is a great and perfect God. His son, Jesus, was sent to earth to die for my sins. If we believe in Him, if we would just believe in Him, we could live for eternity. This life is only temporary, but the next one is perfect. We will see our loved ones, if they believe. Like me, I'll see my brother and daughter and hear her beautiful laugh forever. Isn't that a good reason to strive to be more like God?

Loving each other shouldn't be so hard. Yet, we sell drugs and kill for no reason. Now, I know that drug dealers are no better than murderers, thieves and even child molesters. This is why I say that drugs like meth, cocaine, heroin, and pills all involved money and at the root there is always -- money. Drugs also change people.

I held down the most beautiful girl, with my own hands, just to take her money to buy drugs. She is the only girl I have ever truly loved. I hate myself sometimes. All that keeps me going is the thought that maybe I can change a few lives with my experiences.

Some days I wonder why it takes so much to make people change. It's taken forever and every bad experience to change me. Now I'm done. I'm like a fighter tapping out. I've been beaten and Jesus is the referee that's finally stopping the fight, I've had enough. Jesus is keeping the world from beating me up some more. But I had to tap out and ask Jesus for help.

The world wasn't in my corner stopping the fight, throwing in the towel. I had to give it up. Now Jesus is my trainer and He's preparing me for my next fight. And boy, I'm fighting a super heavyweight who's undefeated and I've lost a few fights to him. This fighter I am up against is called Satan.

The only way to beat this guy is with preparation. A good foundation with Jesus, the greatest trainer. To beat Satan, you have to live like Jesus. You need to get down low on to your knees and ask Jesus for His help. If you can do that you'll win. Me, I am preparing not to lose, but also for a first round knockout. Just because I win the first one doesn't mean there's not going to be a rematch. But at least it will be one win under my belt.

You can have your first win by dropping down to your knees and praying: "Please Lord Jesus, help me." And He will, I know He helped me. I'm finally happy with me and that's the first win I've ever had. It feels amazing. I'm not worried about this world; just getting through and looking at the bright side is enough for me. Some say the bright side doesn't exist at the end of all the bad.

Well, how about this? At the end of my life, there will be Heaven. I'll chill with angels and play hide and go seek in the clouds with my baby girl. I'll play football with my brother, the Preacher and friends. And when Tim Tebow gets there, he'll be our quarterback. No more mountains to climb with armor all over. No more jail cells and loneliness. No more tears. No more hurt. No more pain. Jesus died so that I could have hope of these things.

I remember a time when all I wanted was drugs, money and women. I thought an expensive necklace was my most important endeavor or getting a nice ride to show off in. Now, I'll take homelessness and a Bible. I had to learn from others to achieve this, but now I see we've all got a lot to learn from each other.

The rich need to learn from the poor. The poor need to learn from the rich. The Christians, Muslims,

Jews, black, white, brown, old and young have to learn from and help each other. I've hung out with all kinds and sold drugs to all kinds. None of us are different in the end. We are all human and we all die. The choice you have is love God and do good or not?

I finally made my choice at 27. I finally decided to give up the street life and gangs. I couldn't have done it without Jesus, the Holy Spirit and the direction of a few special people. You've got to direct others to God if you are in Christ because some will be like me and will be unable to change alone. So, help the weak, the dealers, users, alcoholics, and the prostitutes.

Let the Spirit shine in you and God will reward you. Even in jail, I'm being rewarded with simple happiness and that's a lot. What would it mean to you if you could truly be content? You could show others that happiness -- true undying happiness. Once you've found it, people want to know where it came from. You get to lead others to that happiness. And each time your happiness will grow because you just saved a soul.

There is no greater reward than saving a tormented soul. The more it happens, the better it feels. Time here on earth is worthless without being able to help others. I mean why else should we wake up, if we can't distribute knowledge of the source of our happiness and lead others to the same smile we are privileged to? I love it.

In jail, I'm asked, "Why are you so happy?" Well, that's easy. It's Jesus. There's nothing better than walking with Jesus. Just the belief that my Savior is waiting on me and guiding me through the ups and downs of life is amazing. I am the most lost soul ever, yet now I'm found. Praise Him, for otherwise I'd be dead and lost for eternity.

If you are lost, find Jesus. He'll lead you. If you are already walking with him, show others the direction, so they can show someone, who can show others. Let's start a fire within the family of God that will never die.

33. A Letter to Jesus

Dear Jesus,

Please forgive me for my pride and for my lack of faith. Lord you know I try but it's hard sometimes to humble myself and have faith in you, not the world. I still find myself questioning your plan even though the Bible teaches me otherwise.

Please help me control my anger toward others who are controlled by the devil instead of You. Those who strike out at me are the ones I should be holding dear, yet I still can't. I have hatred for the ones who have hurt me in my past, yet You teach me this is wrong. I struggle with that everyday. Please guide me through the trials and tribulations Satan throws my way.

My Lord, only You are worthy of praise. You are the Father of all that is good and holy. Without your sacrifice I am not able to enter the kingdom of Heaven. Please watch over me and guide me so that one day I may enter your kingdom with my brother and daughter. Let angels watch over me and protect me so I'm not tempted towards evil and guide me away when I am. All this I pray in Jesus' holy name. Amen.

PART TWO:

REFLECTIONS

ON

THE LONG

HARD ROAD

34. Reflections

by Ricky Lamar

I am still in jail. This is after my huge transformation, after the Holy Spirit made me reborn, after I gave up the things and thoughts I hold dear or used to hold dear.

It is January, 2012, but I am happy, not upset, and not stressed about how much time I'll get. I am just happy to have God on my side. Life is weird. One day you can't let go of the hurt, the next you are smiling like happiness is all around you.

I've met so many people who have read my story and said it truly changed their lives. Knowing that my story helped them truly blesses me. I had visits and I'm planning on attending a Theology school so I can get closer to God and into youth ministry. I want to stop this cycle of drugs, gangs, and hate. One person can make a difference, even a small one is better than none.

Maybe one day I will meet all of you who read this book in Heaven, because I'm going to be there. Let's drink some sweet iced tea together. I'm dedicating the rest of my life to saving souls.

I no longer hear voices and visions that tell me that I should have saved my brother and daughter. I did all this without medication. That's my biggest blessing and it means a lot to sleep well. I get on my knees to pray and it makes me clean. I'm trying to end my cussing because it turns believers away. I'm writing more books dedicated to God's holy design, so maybe I can save souls that way.

I've read a story about George Medley, who did change from sin to God. I decided to model my life after him. George Medley did what I want to do; left the drugs and he now has a church. That's a more amazing thing than I could dream before, but now I dream and hope to change it all; get visitation of my son and never see another drug again.

I want to work with my kind; drug dealers, killers, and even child molesters, because we all need another chance, no matter how many we've already had. I believe wholeheartedly and without question, "Judge not lest you be judged."

This has been a real healing process for me and I cannot imagine where I'd be without this book project. I feel great, happy, and want healing for everybody. I am trying to change my life one day at a time -- for me, one word at a time.

So, I'll pray for you and you pray for me. I hope I've helped you put things into some perspective because life is not easy. It's not the end either. It's just the long hard road to Heaven.

"Time served." and "I love you, Daddy." I wasn't expecting to hear either phrase, and yet I recently heard both by God's grace. First, after not speaking to my son or his mom for two years, I finally contacted them by phone. I was completely shocked to hear my son say, "I love you, Daddy. I miss you." I last saw him at the age of two years old. He shouldn't even remember me, but by God's grace, I will get to be in his life in the near future.

Then, one week later, the judge deliberated on my case and ordered: "time served." This means that I will receive credit for the jail time I have served and no additional jail time was ordered by the judge. I was fully prepared and even requested to plead out to prison. God can do anything, truly anything, and that includes bringing freedom to you when you think it's impossible.

The happiness that I've felt this week is unsurpassed. The praise I feel goes only to God, no one else. He moved my son's mom to communicate with me. He kept the memory of me in my son's mind alive. He moved the judge to release me. I am now waiting for the court resolution from a minor charge in another State. Pretty amazing! Six months ago, I was looking at life. Now, I am almost free, and getting closer to freedom everyday.

"Lord, I give you the glory and ask that you be with me for all time. I ask that you watch over me and guide me, because without you, there is no love, life, or mercy, so lead me through life with your brightness shining through me."

35. My Reflections

by Yong Hui McDonald

1) An Assignment

Ricky finished his own book, *The Long Hard Road,* which was published in March 2012. I also gathered stories and finished a book, *Tornadoes of War, Inspirational Stories of Veterans and Veteran's Families* and it was published in April 2012.

Then God gave me another assignment, asking me to write a testimony describing Ricky's story of transformation. My first reaction was resistance. His book was already published and I didn't see why I should write about his story.

Then, the Lord reminded me of how He had given me dreams, visions, and how He asked me to help Ricky. I have ministered to many people but somehow the Lord was helping me to understand Ricky's spiritual condition more than any other persons. The Lord convinced me that I am a witness of God's grace which is something I needed to share with others.

When I finally decided to obey the Lord and write my own reflection, the Holy Spirit guided me to gather the stories of other people who also saw Ricky's transformation. In the process, I was so blessed and understood why I had to write this reflection. Ricky's story is an extraordinary story. Without God's power and intervention, Ricky would still live in misery and pain. The Lord blessed him with healing and in the process many others were transformed, and I am one of them.

Now I have more confidence in the Lord's healing power. If Ricky can be healed, I believe anyone can be healed by God's power. Therefore, I give glory to our Lord Jesus for guiding me to write this reflection.

2) Lost

When I met Ricky in the medical unit for the first time in September 2011, I asked him if he needed a Bible or some religious books. As a Chaplain, that's what I do especially since the medical unit doesn't have any religious programs available for patients while they are housed there.

My first impression of Ricky was, "He seems so lost and he is hurting. Here is a man in need of God's healing."

Ricky was smiling and said, "Today, I feel God blessed me so much more than any other time in my life. I thought I would be in prison for a long time, but God favored me and helped me, so I may not be in jail that long. I feel like God is truly alive."

He was beaming, but I still felt sadness in his eyes. He then added, "Oh, I would like to have a Bible."

I was encouraged, thinking to myself, "That's great. God may be able to help him." I gave him a Bible.

He added, "I was a POW in Afghanistan."

"Are you a veteran? I am gathering stories for a veterans' book. Would you like to write your story?" I asked if he wanted to talk about it, and he said he would. When he came out of his room, he explained that he was a former Army Ranger. I grew up in Korea and I am not familiar with American military so I didn't even know what an Army Ranger did. He explained that most of his jobs were in battle and he killed many people while he was in the military.

He said, "I always wanted to write a book. I met a man, we called him Preacher. He was not a chaplain, he was an Army Ranger like me. While on a mission in Afghanistan, he was captured, he became a POW, and died in captivity. When we found him, he had been beheaded. The only way we could identify him was by the cross tattoo on his chest. When I was a POW, I found the Scripture Romans 8:31-39 inscribed in the wall where I was captured. I knew that Preacher wrote it since that was his favorite Scripture. That's what he read to me when he first read the Scripture. My twin brother, J, who also was an Army Ranger, died when he came to rescue me."

The next thing I heard was more horrifying than anything I could imagine.

Ricky said, "My seven year old daughter was kidnapped, raped and killed about a year ago."

I couldn't believe what I heard. I saw tears in this man's eyes. His voice was cracking and he was trying hard to hold back his tears.

I said, "I am sorry about your loss." As I was looking at this man, I was thinking, "Oh, my God, how can this man experience healing? He lost his best friend, his brother in war, and his daughter in a brutal murder. No wonder he looked so lost."

Ricky had a lot of healing to do. Then he shared something I found startling.

He said, "I started praying because I was alarmed when I started conversing with my daughter. I see visions of her and she has been telling me that I wasn't there to protect her. Also, I have visions of my brother who was telling me that he saved me, but I couldn't save him. I have been having nightmares, and I am terrified to go to sleep."

This man's broken heart was caused by the loss of his loved ones, and to make matters worse, he was experiencing accusing visions and voices.

I said, "You have a lot to process. Why don't you write one story at a time so you can start processing your grief and loss? Unless you process them, there is no way you can be freed. I used to suffer from visions of demons and was scared by them, and I was terrified to go to sleep for a long time because of nightmares but God healed me. So, keep praying and the writing will help you."

Ricky used scrap paper to write his story. At this point, I wasn't sure how soon his healing would manifest itself but I knew as he wrote, God would bring healing in his heart. That's what happened to many others I had ministered to over the years. As people start to reflect on their life, the Holy Spirit will give them understanding and start the process of healing.

After I talked to Ricky, I read Romans 8:31-39. As I was reading it, I felt the Holy Spirit's anointing in that Scripture and I started weeping. I have read that Scripture before but this is the first time I felt like I could almost understand how soldiers in battle may have felt and how it would give them courage in the worst situation. I was amazed by the Lord's anointing in that Scripture.

3) Tornadoes, Lessons, and Teachings

In my counseling, I try to understand people from a model that I have developed. It is called the TLT (Tornadoes, Lessons, and Teachings) Model to help others to process their grief and pain.

Any kind of event that produces negative emotional responses, grief, and pain, I call them tornadoes. Until we process our negative emotions and learn lessons from them, we will be stuck in pain.

The worst thing is that the tornadoes we have encountered may produce other tornadoes if we don't process them. People who found peace in the midst of the tornadoes in life are the ones who processed their hurts caused by tornadoes, learned the lessons, and started teaching others.

Every time I listen to the stories of others, I try to understand what stage they are in. If they are in the tornado stage, they feel much pain and turmoil and they feel stuck. If they started processing different areas and start learning lessons from them, their pain will be lessened. When they process all of the areas that caused pain and grief, they can be healed from pain and teach others about the lessons that they have learned.

In this TLT Model, I discovered that writing can facilitate healing. So, I encourage people to write their hurts and pains caused by tornadoes of life. As people write and reflect on the lessons, God can help them see the big picture of what is happening. This can bring healing and they can move on.

Where was Ricky? He was in the midst of the tornadoes of grief and pain. He was stuck and didn't know how to move on from his tragic events. Incarceration is one of his tornadoes caused by not being able to process his hurts and pain. But I knew there was hope for him when he was willing to work on a writing project. I knew God could intervene and bring healing to his broken heart as he writes and spends time on reflection.

Note: To learn more about the TLT Model, read the book, *Tornadoes, Grief, Loss, Trauma, and PTSD: Tornadoes, Lessons and Teachings—The TLT Model for Healing.*

4) Drugs

Soon after I met Ricky, I had a dream about him. In a dream he was lying down and dying. His friend was spoon feeding Ricky drugs, which was actually poison, and he was taking it.

This I believe is what was happening to him when he was in the drug world. It also seemed to be a warning to him that this is what could happen if he goes back to his old friends and a life of drugs. I told him about this dream.

He said, "That could happen."

I felt Ricky wasn't quite convinced of the danger of drugs and I believe that's the reason why God gave me that dream. He was so used to that lifestyle. He mentioned nightmares about drugs. I told him that learning to follow Jesus was the first step to humbling himself. He needed to follow Christ, not the world or his own desires, or drugs that can destroy his mind and life.

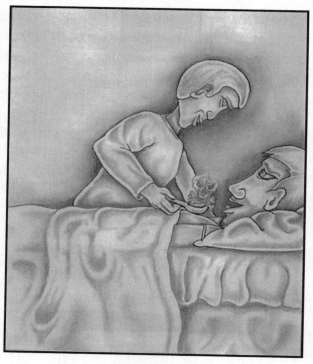

"Drugs"
by Adam Steven Torres

He told me that he would try and I knew Ricky wasn't fully committed to the Lord. It took a while for him to recognize that the lifestyle he was living brought only pain and destruction. I knew it was going to be a gradual process of healing because he wasn't ready to change.

5) Tornadoes

The Lord gave me a vision of Ricky being thrown into the air. When he was about to fall to the ground, God's big hands caught him.

Ricky mentioned that he felt like his incarceration probably saved his life. He said he was selling drugs for a long time, but he didn't start using until his daughter was murdered. He was in so much pain and drugs were how he dealt with his pain. He shared the fact that he lived not caring about life, but with a death wish. Using drugs and selling drugs only lead him to a more destructive lifestyle. That's how he ended up in jail; not knowing what would happen to him in the future. He knew he wouldn't have, or couldn't have changed his life of drugs and gangs if he wasn't incarcerated. Incarceration was a life saving blessing for his life.

"Tornadoes of Grief and Loss"
by Adam Steven Torres

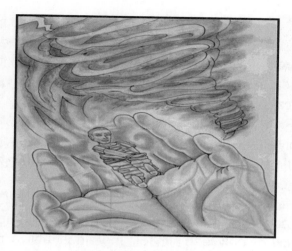

"In God's Hands"
by Adam Steven Torres

6) Forgiveness

Ricky had many issues he had to process, and one of them was forgiveness. He had a difficult time dealing with child molesters in jail.

He said, "I have three child molesters in my pod and I am having a difficult time dealing with that."

I replied, "You have to ask the Lord to help you forgive everyone, including the man who raped and murdered your daughter. Until you do that, you cannot function. As long as you hold on to anger and bitterness, you cannot experience healing or have peace of mind, so, you have to make a decision to forgive."

He wasn't quite ready at that point. Later, however, he said he was thinking about writing a letter to the man who murdered his daughter.

That was a sign of progress but he still had so many areas of forgiveness to deal with. He said he had a difficult time forgiving himself, because he couldn't help his brother or his daughter. Ricky's writing started to help him, but I knew that he had to completely let go of his brother and daughter to heal. I asked him to write a good-bye letter to his brother and daughter. Ricky was trying really hard to process his hurt and pain. After I read his letter to his brother, I was flooded with tears.

7) On The Stage

As he was writing, Ricky struggled because of tormenting visions and voices in the medical unit. I kept telling him that God will bring healing from the hurtful visions and from the nightmares as he gets closer to the Lord. I kept praying for his healing.

"On the Stage"
by Adam Steven Torres

One day the Lord gave me a vision of Ricky standing on the stage, speaking to people. I am seeing him from the back. In addition, the Lord showed me Ricky wearing a black suit, as if he was directing something. God gave me an understanding of how He will use Ricky in the future.

8) Anointing

Ricky finished the short version of his story. His story was powerful. For the first time in my life, I understood the pain of veterans. I have read books and watched movies, but I had not been able to fully comprehend the suffering and pain that veterans of war were going through until I read Ricky's story. I wept while I was reading his story.

He had paid the price of anointing through the pain and grief he had gone through. God knew how much he was hurting and it was only a matter of time before Ricky would be healed from his grief and pain.

I was convinced that the Lord was going to use his story to reach out to many people all over the world. Originally, I was only thinking about a short story about Ricky to go into the veterans book. After I read his powerful story, I told him he should write his own book to help others.

The Holy Spirit directed me to share Ricky's story in worship services. His story touched so many and brought a sense of healing to them. As far as I can remember, his story touched me more than any other story I have read. I started sharing it on the outside as well. The response was amazing. People were deeply touched by his story.

9) Calling

As time passed, the Lord told me Ricky was being called to the ministry. "He started serving me but he doesn't even know it."

I learned that Ricky has the heart of a pastor. He was leading a Bible study and a prayer meeting in the pod whenever he could. But he kept getting into trouble because of fighting. He still had problems dealing with child molesters because he hadn't forgiven them. He had not been able to process his forgiveness and anger issues and many times he was sent to the hole, which is a small solitary room for disciplinary purposes.

Interestingly, he was ministering to people in the hole. When he was given time out of his cell, which was one hour a day, he was sharing his story with others and they were touched by it.

Ricky said others called him Preacher. I knew he was ministering to others and others who had encountered him had told me so. He was very convincing in leading others to see that the Lord was real. I have seen how he was kind and gentle with others who needed encouragement. He knew what others were going through because many came from a similar background of drugs and abuse.

He continued to reach out to others whenever he could and he also helped me with someone that I had a difficult time reaching out to. I had a hard time reaching out to one inmate in the hole and I knew Ricky could reach out to him. I asked Ricky to help him and I thank God that he was able to. Subsequently this man started writing his own story. Praise God!

10) Voices

Ricky continuously had a rough time in jail because he hadn't dealt with his anger and unforgiveness. He shared that he had a problem with authority because the man who raped him was a school superintendent. When he got into a fight, just before he was sent to the hole, I met him in the medical unit. He was in a fine mood. He said since he would be alone, he could focus on writing his stories and that his goal was to finish his book soon.

On December 4, 2011, when Ricky was in the hole the third day, God reminded me about voices and told me to visit him. Many others suffer from voices, but this was the first time the Lord was asking me to visit someone specifically because of hearing voices.

I resisted at first, I had my plan to visit other modules, but decided to ask for a confirmation if that was what the Lord wanted me to do. Immediately, the Holy Spirit gave me the Scripture: *"Anyone, then, who knows the good he ought to do and doesn't do it, sins."* *(James 4:17)*

I was surprised by the response I got. I knew it was the Holy Spirit giving me the Scripture, but I wasn't willing. Throughout the day I became busy and like Gideon, I asked the Lord for another confirmation. I told God that Ricky can request to see me. I didn't get that confirmation, but the Holy Spirit's message came to me stronger than ever. I finally said to myself, "If it was the Holy Spirit, God will show me if Ricky really needed help."

I went to A Module and told the deputy that I wanted to see Ricky because he mentioned to me that he was having problems with hearing voices.

The deputy said, "I was doing room checks just a little while ago, and he told me he was troubled because he was hearing voices of his daughter. That's really odd, as soon as he says it, here the Chaplain shows up."

I said, "Actually visiting him is not my plan but the Holy Spirit told me I have to visit him because he is having a difficult time with hearing voices."

They called Ricky out and he looked more disturbed than any other time I had visited him. He described his daughter appearing in his room, continuously asking him why he wasn't there to protect her, and asking him to bond out which means he would be going back to his old ways. He said he could bond out, but he decided to change his ways, and didn't want to call his drug buddies.

He couldn't read the Bible in the hole and he was constantly bothered by the spirit of his daughter. He was tormented by seeing visions of what happened to his daughter over and over. He couldn't stop the voices or visions of her in that small room.

He said, "I feel like I want to hit the wall, but I know I don't want to break all the bones in my hand. In that small room, I cannot avoid her. I see her in everything."

He was asking to be in medical because that might help him to deal with the distress of seeing and hearing his daughter's voice. I asked, "Do you see your daughter right now?"

He pointed at my right side and said, "She is right there."

I explained, "That's not her. Your daughter is with the Lord and what you are seeing is a spirit disguising itself to look like your daughter."

I called the deputy and I asked Ricky to explain what he was going through. The deputy who heard what was happening realized that Ricky was not safe to be alone, so she made an arrangement for him to be moved to the medical unit.

I said to Ricky, "After you are healed from all of the tormenting voices and visions, you need to write a book to help others who are suffering like you."

Before I left work, I went to medical to check on Ricky. He was in the suicide observation unit and I was able to talk to him through a small window.

He said he was not suicidal, but he would rather be in the suicide unit than stay in the small room where he felt like he was losing his mind. He said he was already feeling better. He could walk around and not be bothered by his daughter's spirit so much.

I told him he might be suffering from claustrophobia and may be unable to handle staying in a small room for a long period of time. He explained that when he was a POW, he was confined in small places and the hole brought back the memories of his trauma, plus he wasn't able to avoid his daughter's spirit in a small room.

I discovered something new from this experience. For people who suffered as POWs and went through torture and trauma, a small room can be a trigger of their painful memories. This is something I didn't know anything about. I talked with him about how he could deal with spiritual encounters. I offered Ricky several coping skills that he could try. He would have to find out what would work for him:

(1) Scripture meditation: since he was in the suicide observation unit, he couldn't have a Bible or any other

papers. I asked him if he memorized any Scriptures. I was surprised to learn that he had memorized quite a few passages of the Bible. I asked him to recite and meditate on the Scriptures as much as possible to fight the voices.

(2) Repent: I asked him to go back in his life and start repenting for his sins from childhood to be right with God. His memory is limited, so he should ask the Holy Spirit to help him repent. He said he had done many wrong things, so he would have many things to repent.

I shared that when I started hearing audible voices, repenting worked for me because at that time I was holding resentment and anger against people. As soon as I told God that I forgave the person and asked for forgiveness for holding the resentment, I didn't hear the voice anymore.

(3) Thank the Lord: Thank God for all the good things He has done. This would help him to focus on the Lord, instead of his problems.

(4) Forgive: He needed to forgive everyone, especially himself. He said forgiving himself would be the hardest one. I told him God forgives us when we ask for forgiveness and in order to find peace in our mind he had to forgive himself.

(5) Repeat the Lord's Prayer: I told him to pray whenever the devil attacked him and made him feel that he was responsible for his daughter's death. It could have happened to anyone and he didn't have any control over what others could do to his daughter. He could repeat, "Deliver us from evil," and focus on God's deliverance.

(6) Not converse with his daughter's spirit anymore: I told him this is not his daughter's spirit because she is with the Lord. She loves her dad and there is no way she

would accuse him or make him feel like he is responsible for her death. The spirit of confusion and torment was after him and he should quit talking as if that was his daughter. He told me that his daughter loved him and there is no way she would hurt him.

(7) Learn to control his thoughts: He needed to be proactive on controlling his thoughts by focusing on God and positive things. Otherwise, he would be inviting wrong thoughts and would end up feeling defeated and would want to hurt himself. That's what the bad spirits want him to do.

I told him that when I am attacked by the spirits, I develop two defenses. The first one is to pray for other people's salvation. The second one is, I ask the Lord to save more people than ever in my ministry. I would like to save more than 20 million people. Whenever the devil attacks me, I raise the number of how many people I would like to save. Ricky was chuckling at that. I told him spiritual war is real and the more we are prepared, we will be able to handle it better.

(8) Be silent and listen to God: Many of the troubles he was experiencing in his mind are caused by listening to wrong voices. He needed to learn to quiet his mind and listen to God's comforting voice. Whenever he hears any bad, negative, and destructive voices, they are coming from the devil, and he needed to resist them and focus on listening to God. I explained that a woman was suffering from voices, but she discovered how to be in silence, control her thoughts, and the voices went away. Ricky said it's hard to quiet his mind.

I said, "It's difficult at first but as you practice more, you will be able to control your thoughts and you can learn to listen. You will have more peace when you practice silence."

(9) Resist the spirit in Jesus' name: I told him about one woman who used to see dark moving objects, when she started resisting them in Jesus' name, they went away and she was healed. I told him he should not accept this vision of his daughter because it's not his daughter. He should resist in Jesus' name because it is a spirit of torment, not from the Lord, but the devil. I told him I used to be troubled by seeing bad spirits which scared me, but I am not afraid of them anymore because I learned to resist them in Jesus' name.

(10) Learn spiritual lessons on how to resist the bad spirits: I told him that he can see this trouble he is going through as a spiritual lesson he has to learn, so when he learns to find peace and not be bothered by spirits, he can teach others. I shared that I suffered from nightmares to the point that I was scared to go to sleep, but God delivered me from it. I don't have nightmares any more. I used to see scary spirits in other people, but as I rely on the Lord for reading of the Scripture and pray more, I was delivered from it. God can deliver him from bad spirits as he learns to rely on the Lord.

(11) Pray for confirmation: I asked Ricky to pray so that God would give him a confirmation that the Lord is taking care of his daughter.

At the end, I prayed for Ricky that God would help him heal from the trauma and flashbacks. I thanked the Lord for asking me to visit him as he indeed was suffering from voices and needed help. I know the Lord is with him and that's why He sent me to see him. Listening to the voice of the Holy Spirit has been a very important part of my spiritual journey. Ricky was going through the purifying fire. This fire is painful, but it's the only path to healing because God teaches us to be humble before Him. Without the Lord's help, we cannot win the spiritual battle or learn how to be humble. Peace is granted to those who are humbled before God and who follow His ways. My prayer at this point was that he would give his heart completely to God's service. The Lord can use his stories of hurt, pain, and tears to bring many people to Christ and healing to those who are hurting.

God can take our weaknesses and turn them into our strengths. When Ricky realizes how to refrain from fighting others, and instead fight the good fight with love and humility, he can learn to love God, love himself, love others and even love child molesters.

Then, and only then, can he be freed from pain and confusion. He will be ready to help many people when he is freed from anger, bitterness, and does not rely on his own strength, but humbly follows the Lord's leading in his life. There were times when I felt my own limitations on how to help him. I knew that only God could bring healing to Ricky who was so shattered by the hurt and pain of his losses. I prayed, "Lord, you have to do it. Ricky cannot do it alone. I cannot do it. You have to intervene and bring healing in his heart."

I have discovered that a little light comes to us at different times and that brings transformation to our hearts. That's God's grace and the Holy Spirit's power working in our lives. We just don't have that power, but the Lord does. Glory to God for Ricky's progress in his spiritual journey even though it is a difficult path for him.

11) Blown Away

On December 7, 2011, four days after Ricky was housed in the medical unit, I went to see him and discovered that he was sent back to the hole in A Module. My first thought was, "How can he handle staying in a small room?"

When I went to A Module, Ricky came out with papers in his hands, which meant he was able to write more stories for his book, I was encouraged. Whenever he wrote, he was able to focus and continue his healing process.

He told me that he wrote some more stories after he met a female trustee in the medical unit. This woman told him that she heard his story in Chaplain's Worship Service and said his story was one of the most touching stories she had ever heard, and it made her cry. She was so happy to meet him face to face.

I already told Ricky about how others were touched by his story, but he couldn't quite understand the extent of it until he heard from her.

Ricky said, "I feel bad that I wasted my time being angry and getting into fights instead of writing my story. After I read how the Holy Spirit led you, and provided you with the steps for healing, I decided to write about how to forgive, step by step, and add it to my book."

"That's a great idea. While you are writing, you will be able to process your forgiveness issue," I replied.

Ricky then shared an amazing dream he had. In his dream, Tim Tebow, Ricky's role model, came to see him and said, "I have read your book and I am going to sponsor you so you can distribute your book freely to the homeless and veterans."

I have seen Ricky smile before, but always with pain in his eyes. This time he was so full of joy and laughter as he was telling me about how this dream encouraged him. I replied, "God is helping you. He is behind you, and He can do so much more than any human being. When your book comes out, you will be surprised how God is going to use it to touch others."

As I left the facility, I was blown away, and at a loss for words. I was so filled with joy in the Holy Spirit and with relief knowing that Ricky found his life's purpose and direction. He had experienced a touch of God's grace. I believe his dream was the work of the Holy Spirit, encouraging him to focus on his writing to glorify God.

"Lord Jesus, thank you. Father God, thank you. Thank you Holy Spirit, you did it again, and so quickly. Just a couple of days ago, I was wondering when Ricky would see the light, but you showed him the light and the way to heal by focusing on helping others. I can't thank you enough. Lord Jesus, I love you. How can I share your greatness with others? Lord Jesus, you are a great God!"

Ricky's book will open people's hearts to see how great God is. Without God's healing power, Ricky's story would be buried in his memory and he would die with the pain of grief and anger. But God's gracious hands caught him just before he crashed to the ground.

The Lord has shown him that there is a better way. Instead of being buried in grief and pain, he can experience healing through God and share His great love and compassion with others. In the process, he will find the joy of serving the Lord, and others who read his story will experience healing through the power of God. I was amazed by what God could do to bring healing to a broken and shattered heart such as Ricky's. I have seen it many times in others but this is another miracle that God has helped me to see. I thank God again for calling me to prison ministry. Praise God!

Ricky said Tim Tebow is his role model. "I want to do what he does. He helps many people. Also, George Medley from ABC Ministries is my role model. I can identify with him more than Tim Tebow because George was incarcerated and used drugs."

George used to be incarcerated at ACDF and he was in and out of jails and prisons. He used drugs and was selling drugs but after he became a Christian, he quit using and started helping others. Ricky said that he wanted to work with George in the future to help others.

I told Ricky three things to remember when he starts doing well and be recognized by other people with his work, especially in his writing. First, give glory to God. Second, humble yourself. Third, be faithful to the Lord. I repeated this over and over so he would understand that God is the one who is helping him in his difficult times, and he needs to keep walking with a humble attitude with God. Only then will he be able to make a difference in other people's lives.

12) Determination

How was Ricky able to continuously write in his tormented state? I can say it was his determination to get his story out and to experience healing. It was through God's grace that his story not only helped him but also encouraged others in their healing process. I encouraged him to keep praying and writing because God can bring healing from the tormenting visions, voices, and nightmares.

God was also helping Ricky through others who had an artistic gift of drawing. Not long after I met Ricky, an inmate told me that he could draw and asked me how he could help me with the book project.

I gave him Ricky's story and asked him to draw whatever that comes to him. He drew some pictures and they were inspirational, but he couldn't figure out what to draw about Ricky's daughter. When Ricky wrote a letter to his brother. The artist read the story and drew a picture of Ricky's brother holding his daughter.

Many times Ricky mentioned how much this drawing of his brother holding his daughter brought so much comfort and healing.

A person who heard about Ricky's story said, "I will help him to make his story into a book, and will not charge him anything. His story can be made into a movie and I can send it to a movie company." This happened when Ricky hadn't even finished the book.

Ricky's story was continuously touching others. A director from Lost and Found where they offer counseling services for veterans who suffer from PTSD and other problems, read Ricky's story. She said, "I am going to put him on the stage. His story was so touching. I majored in Theater and I can write the play script for Ricky."

Others who read Ricky's story from the outside started writing and visiting him, and they gave him much encouragement. Ricky was amazed by the reactions of others who read his story.

He said, "I am so filled with joy. I never expected that I would have this much joy in my life."

It was the Holy Spirit's joy he was feeling. God blessed him through others who recognized Ricky's gifts of writing and the pain he went through.

Ricky said, "I never liked writing, but now I enjoy writing. I was writing to help myself so I can be released from emotional pain, but I never expected that my story would touch that many people."

13) A Heavenly Vision

Ricky was slowly recovering from grief and loss, but the ultimate healing came when he had a vision of his loved ones who told him they were doing fine. This vision changed his life. Interestingly, he had this vision as he was holding the drawing of his brother holding his daughter in heaven. Thanks to the artist and God who gave this heavenly vision to bring healing to Ricky.

Ricky's vision of his loved ones in heaven is truly a blessing and an answer to his prayers. He couldn't accept the death of his brother and his daughter as a part of life's journey before he had this vision. After he had this vision, his attitude changed. He wrote that even in death there is hope because we have hope of seeing our loved ones in heaven.

Not long after he had this vision, he told me he didn't have any tormenting visions, voices, or nightmares anymore. He said he was not scared to go to sleep anymore and was not suffering from pain but has joy. He said he wasn't taking medication for visions or nightmares, so he knew the Lord brought healing. Ricky was smiling. He was a changed man after that. I knew his healing came from no one else, but the Lord. I knew no one could do it but the Lord can heal and free us from tormenting visions, voices, and nightmares.

I was so thankful that God brought healing to Ricky. I knew healing would come if he kept growing spiritually and in his relationship with the Lord. Actually, I didn't expect that his healing would happen that fast. I knew the Lord could bring instant healing, so I shouldn't be surprised, but Ricky had so many issues.

He was able to finish his book and said, "I want to be like you. I want to write many books to help many people."

I replied, "If you keep following the Lord, the Holy Spirit will guide your writing, and you will be able to write many books." Ricky was very open in sharing about his hurts and feelings. That's one of the reasons why he was able to write a powerful book.

14) Shaking

I was praying and the Lord gave me a vision that Ricky was in God's hands. The Lord's hands started shaking, Ricky was stumbling, and powder started coming out of his pants pockets. This vision was telling me that God was shaking Ricky to become clean. He experienced healing from nightmares, tormenting voices and visions but he still had many areas that needed healing.

I told Ricky about the vision God had given me and asked him if there was anything that he needed to change. He mentioned that it means he was relying on prescription drugs and that's what he needs to let go of.

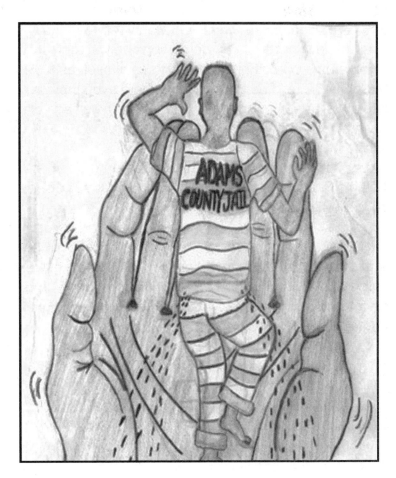

"Shaking"
by Scott Martinez

That was only one area but he had many areas that needed cleansing and change. One of those areas was patience. He struggled with daily life at the jail. He had a difficult time dealing with others who didn't have much respect for anyone. Ricky was a strong person and with his military training, he could fight. The whole time I saw him, he carried himself with dignity and self-respect.

I knew that's one of the reasons he was getting into more trouble with others. He didn't see himself as a person who could be trampled by others even though he was an inmate. He also had respect for others regardless of who they were. But he couldn't stand people who were putting others down and challenging him.

Ricky said he was constantly bothered by others in the pod. He kept moving from the pod because of that. He looked troubled.

He said, "After I told others that I was done with gangs and drugs, a man was constantly calling me names and challenging me. I hit him. That was a mistake. I used to feel good if I hit someone who challenged me, but for the first time in my life, I felt so bad. I knew it was God telling me I shouldn't have done that."

I said, "That's great. you finally feel the conviction of the Holy Spirit. If you didn't feel bad, you would be doing it again, so it's good that you felt bad about it."

Ricky said, "I am not going to get into fights anymore."

When he was leading a Bible study, he had many challenges with others who didn't think he should associate with people of colors. Ricky asked the deputies to move him to a different pod because he didn't want to get into fights with others anymore.

Some deputies told him to fend for himself, but Ricky didn't want to get into a fight. I saw him asking deputies at least three times, but he may have asked more. He kept asking and he was glad when he was moved to another pod.

He told me he learned a lesson through this. He said, "The Lord was testing me to see if I could hold my temper and not fight. When I finally learned how to hold my temper, He moved me."

He also mentioned that it was three times harder to share Christ with others in the jail, so he decided to withdraw from trying to lead the Bible study after he moved to the other pod. It seemed he was content for a while then I saw him becoming restless. He said he was tired and the desire to leave the jail had become so strong. I saw him struggling with an anxious and discontented spirit more than ever. He told me what's difficult is that he hated being in jail, and with one phone call, he could be out. I knew God didn't plan for him to leave the jail with the help of his drug buddies.

This actually was a necessary process for him because temptations will always be there. When he is outside of the jail, the temptation to go back to his old life would be much greater because there is nothing that will hold him back. Incarceration was a good thing since he still had the urge to follow his old ways. This is a cleansing and purifying process for him and he will have to struggle with this urge until he commits one hundred percent to follow Jesus.

15) Praying

I was concerned about Ricky's condition of restlessness. Just before I went to see him, the Lord gave me a vision that Ricky was praying in God's hands. When I visited Ricky, the first words he said was, "I have been praying." He came out with some papers in his hands which meant he was focusing on positive things. Whenever he writes, the Holy Spirit blesses him and Ricky is happy and filled with joy from the Lord.

I said, "God has clearly shown me that your desire to bond out is not God's plan, but it is coming from your own desire and you have to let God help you." He agreed with me. I explained, "The Lord has given me the Scriptures to tell you." I told him the following Scriptures:

(1) *"Then he said to them all: 'If anyone would come after me, he must deny himself and take up his cross daily and follow me. For whoever wants to save his life will lose it, but whoever loses his life for me will save it. What good is it for a man to gain the whole world, and yet lose or forfeit his very self? If anyone is ashamed of me and my words, the Son of Man will be ashamed of him when he comes in his glory and in the glory of the Father and of the holy angels.'"* (Luke 9:23-26)

(2) *"To keep me from becoming conceited because of these surpassingly great revelations, there was given me a thorn in my flesh, a messenger of Satan, to torment me. Three times I pleaded with the Lord to take it away from me. But he said to me, 'My grace is sufficient for you, for my power is made perfect in weakness.' Therefore I will boast all the more gladly about my weaknesses, so that Christ's power may rest on me. That is why, for Christ's sake, I delight in weaknesses, in insults, in hardships, in persecutions, in difficulties. For when I am weak, then I am strong."* (2 Corinthians 12:7-10)

"Praying"
by Scott Martinez

16) Humility

Ricky said that he realized he could not go back to his old friends so he started writing more. He read the story he had written, "Fight," and I felt the Lord's presence. God has anointed his story and the Lord was helping me to experience this anointing. This doesn't happen very often, but it happened with his writing.

God was blessing Ricky's desire to serve the Lord instead of following his desires which would lead him to more pain and destruction. He made a decision to follow the Lord not his own desires. I warned him if he ever goes back to using drugs, he would suffer greatly because he will be vulnerable to the same tormenting visions and voices.

He had already suffered from it and doesn't have to go back to that painful condition. This sounds harsh, but it's a reality. Many people who have gone back to the drug world have found out that they put themselves in the worst condition ever. Of course the Lord will forgive them when they turn to Him, but they will be paying the price of falling away, living in pain, and it's not worth it.

17) The Robe

I had a vision of Ricky wearing a minister's robe, and it was not made from earthly material. It was gold in color and red on the back. His devotion to serve the Lord was evident, although not everyone was recognizing it.

I had a vision of a minister's gown in my dreams only one other time with a woman pastor. This is the second time God was showing me a person wearing a minister's gown—heavenly gown. He was leading Bible study and learning to forgive others, while ministering to others.

I knew he had a difficult time with child molesters in the jail, but God started healing his unforgiving heart. He said he understood that drug dealers are not any better than child molesters and everyone deserves another chance.

That was a miracle. He finally saw the light. That's God's grace! God helped him to see the reality that everyone is a sinner before God. Without forgiveness, he cannot be healed, but will be immobilized with pain. He was getting it. He actually seemed to be surprised by the change in his attitude as well.

He said, "I was playing basketball with them and I feel fine." He was smiling.

I thanked God for helping him to forgive. Ricky mentioned that he felt it's wrong to think that children who were molested by others would turn into child molesters. He said he never had that kind of desire and couldn't understand how a person who knew the pain of being molested could molest another child and make them go through the same pain. He mentioned this while in a group discussion, a man said that because he was molested as a child, he himself became a molester.

Ricky immediately disagreed with the man and said, "I was molested, but I didn't become a child molester. If you know how much pain you have gone through, why would you put others through that pain. You are using that as an excuse. You have to take responsibility for your action. You made that decision and shouldn't use your past as a crutch."

He was very vocal about his molestation and other misconceptions about people who were molested. He told me he would eventually write a book on how he was molested to help others.

I told him that would be a good idea. I was very glad to see that Ricky was able to change his hateful feelings toward child molesters. Before he saw every child molester as his object of hate and anger. But now, he sees them with a different set of eyes. I was very happy to see his progress in this matter.

Only God can help us to see our spiritual condition, acknowledge we are all sinners and realize that no one is any better than the person next to him. We may not make the same mistake as others, but that doesn't make us any different before the Lord. The only difference is some of us are forgiven because we ask for forgiveness.

18) Dancing

The Lord gave me a vision of Ricky dancing in God's hands. God asked me to write my reflection on Ricky's transformation. He also told me to ask Ricky to write how much God loved him through other people.

Actually, when the Lord gave me this vision, I was skeptical. How can he be happy to the point of dancing? The last time I saw him was when God asked me to go and pray for him. I found him in the medical unit, he came out holding his stomach. He was in pain. He was having a difficult time carrying on a conversation.

Ricky was in the medical unit often because of his physical pain. At that time he told me he was given only pain medication and liquids for five days to heal his body. So, I wondered how he could be dancing. The Lord already knew what was happening to him. I was surprised to find out that indeed, he was so filled with joy, more than ever before.

When I visited Ricky he told me that he contacted his wife and son on the phone. They were asking him to come home and be a dad.

He told me that his son said, "I love you daddy." "He said he wanted to go fishing with me. Today, I felt so much of God's love. More than when I finished the book, and more than any other time in my life."

He couldn't stop telling me how loved he felt by his son. Ricky was filled with joy—so much more than any other time I had ever seen him. He said that it was all coming from the Lord. Ricky mentioned that his wife and his family didn't do drugs and they are good people. The reason they couldn't be with him was because he was involved in drugs. Now, he decided not to go back to drugs and they are ready to have him back.

The Lord did it again, He showed His grace and Ricky prayed the most touching and humble prayer of thanksgiving and dedication to God's service. I told him God gave me a vision of Ricky dancing in the Lord's hands and He asked me to ask him to write how much God loved him through others. I asked if he would write how he felt that day—God's love and all he was feeling. He said he would. I reminded him of the Scripture. *"Jesus replied, 'No one who puts his hand to the plow and looks back is fit for service in the kingdom of God.'"* (Luke 9:62) I also told him that God was telling me that Ricky would not be in this facility too long. His court date is coming up and he may be leaving soon if everything goes right.

"Dancing"
by Adam Steven Torres

Ricky said when he gets out, he is planning to attend a Bible college, get a doctorate degree, and write many books. I told him that's a great goal to have. Ricky humbled himself and God blessed him with another chance to make it with his family. *"If my people, who are called by my name, will humble themselves and pray and seek my face and turn from their wicked ways, then will I hear from heaven and will forgive their sin and will heal their land." (2 Chronicles 7:14)*

19) The Armor

I had a vision of Ricky in God's hands and this time he was wearing armor, holding a sword, and practicing how to use it.

"The Armor"
by Adam Steven Torres

This was two days before his court date. I was actually in disbelief. The next day I visited him and the Lord had confirmed to me that what He showed me was really happening. Ricky came out with a big smile and he was telling me how he was comparing the photo on his I.D. card when he first came to ACDF with the present time. Now he can smile. He had a big smile and I asked him how he was doing.

"I have been reading the Bible, meditating on lots of Scriptures, and that helps me. In addition, I had a dream last night that I was fishing with my son. I was catching a fish and it was the best dream."

I said, "That will happen in the future and I am glad that you are doing well."

His joy was coming from the Lord. He was learning to focus on the Lord by reading the Scripture. Ricky said some people were asking him why he was so happy. He would tell them, "I know it's the Lord." God showed him favor. I know this is happening to many inmates who have gone through a lot, but learn to rely on the Lord. I prayed with him, and when I left, I was filled with joy of the Holy Spirit.

20) Grace

One of the areas Ricky had to process was to let go of blame and anger toward God after he lost his loved ones. He mentioned that he lived with anger and hatred toward God especially when he lost his daughter. How could a good and loving God allow things like that to happen to his daughter?

What he didn't see at that time was that God is not responsible for pain caused by other people. It took a while for him to process it and finally understand that we do have a good and loving God who cares about us.

He began to thank God in many ways, but when he was able to talk to his son, and received good news from the court, he seemed to understand God's love more than any other time in his life. Ricky wrote a wonderful testimony of how he felt God's love through his son.

21) Lessons

I learned many lessons from the encounter with Ricky.

God's mercy was shown to Ricky — When Ricky was upset and angry at God, he was rebellious. His use of drugs and selling drugs was a part of his rebellious spirit working within him. The Lord knew he was hurting and needed healing from his grief and pain. All it took was Ricky to humble himself and turn to God for healing. God showed mercy and brought healing in him.

Ricky's healing was a process — Ricky's healing didn't come over night but with a gradual process. He was willing to work hard to process his hurt and pains. He had many issues to be resolved and he had to make changes in attitudes and actions with the help of God. When he started to process unforgiveness, anger, and letting go, he started feeling better. His ultimate healing came when the Holy Spirit blessed him with a heavenly vision. He was able to accept the loss of his loved ones and have hope of seeing them in the future. He received answers for his prayers. He didn't suffer from emotional pain any more. He could focus on living in the present and not in the past. We have our own part to work on in order to process grief and loss. Ricky worked on them diligently.

The Lord has performed a miracle in Ricky's life. — The most significant healing is that he is not seeing any traumatic visions of his daughter or his brother telling him that he should have saved them. Also, he is not suffering from nightmares anymore. Ricky was able to smile with no sadness or pain in his eyes. He couldn't do that on his own. Only God can do that.

God's grace is sufficient in any circumstance even in jail — While Ricky was going through so much pain and anguish in jail, he was able to finish his book which not only helped him process his healing, but also helped others who needed healing.

He found new direction — He was directionless when he came to jail. After he was healed, he found a new direction to help others. Because of what he has gone through Ricky understands others' pain and hurt. He also knows Jesus can help. God gave him another chance to prove that he can make a difference in the world where there are many hurting people.

God wants our testimonies to be shared to give Him glory — I have seen many miracles in my ministry. Ricky's story is one story that God has blessed me with. I am thankful that the Lord told me to write what I have witnessed; God's healing power freed Ricky from torment and pain and people need to hear about it.

I see hope in every situation —I have met many who are grieving from the loss of their loved ones, but I have not met anyone who had gone through more than Ricky. I know no one but God can heal a person who was broken as much as Ricky was. His healing story blessed me with a sense of hope. God could heal a person who seemed to be beyond repair.

A while back, I told God I wanted to see more healing in my ministry. He said, "Unless you understand the pain of others, you cannot bring healing." That makes sense to me. Unless I understand others' hurts and pain, I wouldn't even try to help them. God taught me about other people's pain through Ricky, especially military people, veterans, homeless and prisoners. Ministering to Ricky was a blessing for me.

Ricky's story is just the beginning — Before Ricky left the facility, I told Ricky how I was pleased with his progress in many areas and his writing, but I consider writing was only 50% of his transformation. The real test is when he gets out of jail. When he can live out what he tries to teach others is the other 50% of transformation. I pray that the Lord will guide his path of transformation.

36. A Story of Transformation

by Deanna Chilton

Meeting Ricky—There is no question—I had a divine appointment awaiting me on two occasions. One was in Sept. 2011 when I met Chaplain Yong Hui McDonald of the Adams County Detention Facility (ACDF). The other came shortly thereafter in meeting one of the inmates there, Ricky.

I had never had a calling from God or anybody else to serve in a prison/jail environment before in my life, until now. In the summer of 2011, my friend had asked me to come help her pass out the bottles of water to the homeless in Denver.

My friend and I, along with my children, began walking and praying in areas in Denver where many homeless gathered.

We met a man and prayed with him to ask Jesus to be with him in his heart. Before leaving he asked if we would visit his daughter in the Denver jail. My friend and I said we would. My friend tried to find this person to no avail. However, in her attempts she was put in contact one day with Chaplain Yong Hui McDonald. She asked if my friend and I would be willing to help with the women's worship at ACDF, and we accepted.

On our second visit to ACDF the Chaplain asked my friend to lead the worship on her own, and asked if I would accompany her to pray with some inmates. We stopped in her office and she had me read a story by an inmate that she needed to visit.

It's funny, I had decided in my mind that I would only serve at ACDF with the women inmates, but God had other plans for me. Now to date (March 2012) I have been serving both the women and the men at ACDF. I have been truly blessed by their stories, sufferings, and feel it is a privilege to pray with my brothers, sisters and those searching.

As I sat in Chaplain McDonald's office and read Ricky's story my heart began to pound, there was a stirring in my Spirit, and tears welled up in my eyes. This story, like very few others, had made such an impact on my heart and soul. It was inspired by the Holy Spirit, and even though it was quite rough in its original state I knew that God had His Hand on this young man and had something amazing in store for his life.

I immediately had a stirring of the Holy Spirit that Ricky's story would be used to share Christ with many, many people. When I first met with Ricky, yes, he had an amazing story to tell, but it seemed he wasn't quite prepared (by God) to tell it.

He was angry, rebellious, lacking peace and blamed his actions and reactions on those around him. I told him God had an amazing plan for his life; that I had read his story and could see God's Hand on him from the beginning.

I asked Ricky what he would say to that young boy in his story, knowing what he knows now. He simply said, "Don't do drugs." I knew Ricky's heart was not ready for the plans God had laid out for him. Also, I knew God would not arrange for Ricky's release from ACDF until He had transformed his life through Christ Jesus. God summoned me to pray for Ricky from that day on. (At the time he was talking about being released in November 2011, which would have been less than a month away).

This was a young man who had a remarkable story of Christ's love for Him to share with the world; however, a couple of key components were missing from Ricky's character— humility and forgiveness.

However, over the next several months when I met with Ricky I was blessed to see his transformation made through Christ Jesus — the One who can transform a heart for Him like nothing we can describe or have the ability to do ourselves. It is, simply put, an unexplainable phenomenon of God.

At first, he was angry and not trusting of anyone around him; struggling with sorrow, guilt, pain and loss (which any of us would be considering all he had experienced in his young life). Over the next few months, though, God would deal head on with these issues.

A couple of months after our first meeting the most dramatic change happened. I had felt God waking me in the middle of the night to pray for Ricky. A verse was given.

"But Samuel replied: 'Does the LORD delight in burnt offerings and sacrifices as much as in obeying the voice of the LORD? To obey is better than sacrifice, and to heed is better than the fat of rams.'" (1 Samuel 15:22)

I found from God this was a verse not only for Ricky but for my own life. (This transpired about a week or so before Christmas 2011).

The following week I visited with Ricky. He was a changed person. His entire demeanor was different. He smiled a lot, he seemed at peace (even though his circumstances had not, nor did it look like they would change), and he seemed to have an inner joy.

He began to tell us what had happened to him. He was put 'in the hole' (solitary confinement), because of fighting.

He was given all his meals in this small cell and only allowed outside the door an hour every day. While he was in there Ricky described voices and images coming to him (a tormenting spirit) matching the description of his young daughter and his brother who were killed.

They were persecuting Ricky, asking him why he didn't save them, blaming him for their murders... Finally, Ricky had cried out to God for deliverance.

A vision was given to him of his daughter and brother with the Preacher who was an Army Ranger; they were fine, happy, at peace, and smiling. They told Ricky that they were fine, they were happy where they were. It was Ricky that was in the hard place, but that he should make his life count.

Ricky realized that this was the truth; that God was speaking truth to him and the previous tormenting spirits were of Satan, who had been speaking lies.

I realized, as Ricky re-told his experiences in 'the hole' God had spoken to me, as well, while Ricky was going through this, God was awaking me in the middle of the night to pray for him. It seemed my prayer took place at the same time frame as Ricky's recent days in solitary confinement.

Since that point on, as I visited Ricky, he exuded joy, kindness, forgiveness, humility, total deliverance and complete devotion to Christ. As I write this, I find it hard to believe myself that such a dramatic change can take place in a person over a relatively short period of time.

If I hadn't witnessed it with my very own eyes, I wouldn't have believed it. It is truly a transformation of a person that God Almighty, Himself, has great plans for and not a lot of time here on earth for it to be gradual. There was no doubt in my mind that this was the work of Christ Jesus in a heart and soul—this dramatic change could not have happened in and of human strength alone.

"My ears had heard of you but now my eyes have seen you." (Job 42:5)

I continue to pray for Ricky because his road does not get easier; Satan does not want a warrior like Ricky in this world, thus, Satan will fight hard to thwart God's plans. But rest assured. If Ricky keeps faithful (and sees his faith grow) and keeps his eyes on Jesus—some things are possible with people, but ALL things are possible with God through the power of Jesus Christ, Ricky's story will have many come to Believe! I wrote this on March 8, 2012.

37. God Opened My Heart

by Julia Tapia

I received Ricky's short story to edit. At 3:00 A.M. as I was reading his story I was unable to edit the words. I was so touched by it because of all the pain he went through. I wondered how a person can go through that much pain and still stand.

I called Yong Hui and told her that I wanted to meet him. Yong Hui had a picture of him from the DVD interview about his military experiences. I broke down and cried when I saw his picture. I saw such an empty vessel. I saw so much pain. I hadn't felt that much pain for years. When I saw his picture, it opened up my heart to love and care. You just wanted to take him, hold him, love him and take the pain away from him just like a mother would. From that point on, I started praying for him everyday and I still do.

About a week or two later, he had a transformation. Instead of me taking his pain away, Jesus got there before me. So, when I had heard this transformation through the Holy Spirit, I visited him at the jail. He was nothing like the picture that I saw.

He was beaming with joy and the glory of God was all over him. He did most of the talking because he was so excited about what happened while he was in solitary confinement where his transformation took place. Just like the Bible says that Moses glowed with the glory of God when he came down from the mountain after spending time with God for forty days, that's the way I saw Ricky with the glory of God all over him.

I just listened and then encouraged. Jesus can take someone like him and transform and give him new life and Ricky wanted to share it.

He said, "Can you believe that I could write a book? I couldn't even write an essay in school."

We conversed and I felt so blessed to have met someone that God had touched firsthand. I felt so privileged in the presence of God's glory and goodness.

I continued to visit him and I write to him. I wrote Scriptures down that I used to send to my own children when they were in prison. Ricky would answer my letters, but I had a difficult time reading them because he was writing with a golf pencil.

I shared Ricky's manuscript with my co-worker. She just read the first chapter and gave me some money to put on Ricky's account. When I asked him if he received the money on the phone, he said, "Yes, I bought some coffee and cookies for my Bible study."

Another time when he called me he was telling me about a young man who came up to him and started arguing with him. The man punched Ricky in the face. Ricky said to him, "Why do you want to fight with me. Come to my cell and I will give you some coffee and you can come to my Bible study."

It made me realize that when God changes you, it's a total transformation. I used to have a temper but God changed me and I saw that God had changed Ricky too. I replied, "*Jesus said, 'Do not resist an evil person. If someone strikes you on the right cheek, turn to him the other also.'* That's what you did. The other cheek was inviting him for coffee and to your Bible study."

I shared Ricky's story with my employer, George Medley, who had started ABC ministries to help the poor. His story came out in the book, *Prisoners Victory Parade*. Ricky read George's story and he was so touched and it encouraged him to write more.

Ricky and George started corresponding and Ricky wanted to meet George. I asked George if he would like to go and meet this young man since Ricky thought so highly of him. George said, "I don't think they will let me in because I was a felon."

I immediately went into prayer and asked the Lord to open the doors so George can see Ricky. We went to visit Ricky and George was able to see him as a visitor on the TV monitor.

George and Ricky talked the whole time and I didn't get to visit him hardly at all. But that was okay because they were having such a good time, sharing the love of God with each other.

When we were about to leave, Ricky asked George to pray for him, so he prayed for him. After we left the jail, we were both speechless because we had spent 30 minutes in the presence of God and saw the transformation that God had done in Ricky.

When Ricky's book came out, when I saw the cover, I embraced the book to my heart and I cried. I still pray for him as a son. When I pray for him I always break down. Through this experience with Ricky, I have learned how to see pain the way God sees it. I learned how to see humanity with love and compassion. This never happened to me with anyone else.

Not only Ricky was transformed, I was transformed also. I learned to care more about the forgotten ones, whether it would be inmates or homeless. I think it's a ripple effect. God transformed him and through him, God transformed me. Today because of my own transformation, I am able to pray for others with compassion and love which I didn't have before. Sometimes our eyes can be open to other people's pain but until your heart is open, you will not have compassion for the forgotten humanity.

Jesus said in His word, *"When he saw the crowds, he had compassion on them, because they were harassed and helpless, like sheep without a shepherd." (Matthew 9:36)* Through meeting Ricky, I became a better intercessor and in that way he has helped me in the ministry.

38. He Walked With His Head Up

by Michelle Lopez

When the judge sentenced me to two years in Adams County Detention Facility, I was devastated. My immediate response was I'm not supposed to be in jail, I am different, I have an education, and a degree. I quickly applied as an inmate worker and received a job in medical. Once again I was disappointed thinking, "Yuck, the people in medical are gross."

I decided to go to work in medical and that's when I first encountered Ricky. He was young, tall, slender, and kind. I also immediately noticed that he was hurting, not physically, but emotionally. He appeared to be broken in several pieces.

Ricky loves to talk "a lot." I would usually just walk away from him thinking, "I wish he'd shut up. I have my own problems." One day I was bored and actually stopped to listen to what he had to say. He talked about sports, politics, and the Army. He began to tell me about his life, starting with his daughter who was raped and killed. I couldn't help but to cry. I mean, that could have been my daughter or any child for that matter.

I remember thinking how strong this guy was. How can he tell this story and not cry? I asked him if he read the Bible and if he prays to God.

He said, "No. He doesn't care about me. I don't even believe that there is a God." I was appalled. I told him that I'd pray for him. Then, I wanted to know why he doesn't believe that our Father heals and performs miracles. So, I asked him and he continued to tell me why he felt this way. Besides losing a daughter, he lost a brother, a wife and didn't have parents that were ever there for him.

"So God hates me if there is one," he said.

I felt so much hurt through his voice and words that I cried for him. The pain that this guy was experiencing was deep. I asked him to pray with me and he agreed. This was the first time I saw Ricky cry. I told him to have faith and don't ever give up.

When he asked to speak with the Chaplain, I was ecstatic to see him talking to her. One day, he was very excited about a new project. Of course, he told me about his life story being told to the Chaplain and that she wants him to write it on paper.

He kept reminding me about paper for writing and wanted me to continuously proof read it for him. He asked for some more paper and even during lock down, he rolled 10 pencils under the door and hand gestured me to sharpen them. Every time I saw him, he had his nose in this paper. Because he used to talk so much, but he was quiet after he started writing, I sometimes had to check if he was still there. I mentioned to him that he's quiet and he said he didn't want to leave out anything.

Then, he said what I never thought he would say. "Michelle, God had helped me because I'm still alive." I told him that God knew he was strong enough to handle what was given to him. I was glad that writing his story on paper reminded him that God really does exist. He started reading Scriptures from the Bible and speaking of the miracles God performs. He walked with his head up and very proud to be a born again Christian. He said that his life story was going to help others. As he had finished with his court appearance he said, "Whatever God's will is, I am ready."

Ricky had transformed a lot during the eight months. He learned to control his anger. He went from not believing to praying on a daily basis. He was dealing with his hurt and pain with the guidance of God.

I thought the best thing was Ricky wanted to make the difference in just one person's life by telling his testimony. Now, he was going to get his story to many people. It was so great for him because now he felt like he "had a purpose." He was so proud of himself for writing his testimony to help others.

Ricky no longer felt insignificant, he was special, and he is a child of God. The last time I saw Ricky he told me that he forgave his mom that she did the best she could, since she was a single mother. He then knew that forgiveness was the key to his happiness.

I have still never told him "Thank you" because I was the first person his story helped. Not only did my life not seem so bad, but I realized that God put Ricky in my path to see that I am just like any other inmate even with an education. Later, I apologized to Ricky for thinking he should shut up and told him that he made me realize that the problems I had were very insignificant to what Ricky had gone through. Thanks to God for bringing Ricky and his story to me.

APPENDICES

Romans 8:31-39

"What, then, shall we say in response to this? If God is for us, who can be against us? He who did not spare his own Son, but gave him up for us all-- how will he not also, along with him, graciously give us all things? Who will bring any charge against those whom God has chosen? It is God who justifies. Who is he that condemns? Christ Jesus, who died--more than that, who was raised to life-- is at the right hand of God and is also interceding for us. Who shall separate us from the love of Christ? Shall trouble or hardship or persecution or famine or nakedness or danger or sword? As it is written: 'For your sake we face death all day long; we are considered as sheep to be slaughtered.' No, in all these things we are more than conquerors through him who loved us. For I am convinced that neither death nor life, neither angels nor demons, neither the present nor the future, nor any powers, neither height nor depth, nor anything else in all creation, will be able to separate us from the love of God that is in Christ Jesus our Lord."

An Invitation

Do you have an empty heart that cannot
be filled with anyone or anything? God can fill
your empty heart with His love and forgiveness.
Do you feel your life has no meaning, no direction,
no purpose, and you don't know where to turn to
find the answers? It's time to turn to God. That's the
only way you will understand the meaning and the
purpose of your life. You will find direction that will
lead you to fulfillment and joy. Is your heart broken
and hurting, and you don't know how to experience
healing? Until we meet Christ in our hearts, we
cannot find the peace and healing that God can
provide. Jesus can help heal your broken heart. If
you don't have a relationship with Christ, this is an
opportunity for you to accept Jesus into your heart
so you can be saved, find peace and healing from
God. Here is a prayer if you want to accept Jesus:

"Dear Jesus, I surrender my life and everything to you.
I give you all my pain, fear, regret, resentment, anger,
worry, and concerns that overwhelm me. I am a
sinner. I need your forgiveness. Please come into my
heart and my life and forgive all my sins. I believe
that you died for my sins and that you have plans
for my life. Please heal my broken heart and bless
me with your peace and joy. Help me to cleanse my
life so I can live a godly life. Help me to understand
your plans for my life and help me to obey you. Fill
me with the Holy Spirit, and guide me so I can follow
your way. I pray this in Jesus' name. Amen."

About The Authors

Ricky Lamar

Sergeant Ricky served as an Army Ranger
in Afghanistan for 3 years. He was a POW and
was honorably discharged on medical grounds in
2005. Ricky experienced many losses in his life. He
lived a hard life of drugs, gangs, and violence. He
experienced an amazing transformation through
God. His story has touched and inspired many
people. He is serving the Lord by preaching to
other prisoners and bringing hope, faith and
transformation. His goal in life is to save souls. He
plans to attend theology school after he is released
and go into youth ministry to stop the cycle of drugs,
gangs, and hatred.

Yong Hui V. McDonald

Yong Hui V. McDonald, a United Methodist
minister, has been working as a chaplain at Adams
County Detention Facility (ACDF) in Brighton,
Colorado, since 2003, and as an on-call hospital
chaplain since 2002. She is a certified American
Correctional Chaplain, spiritual director, author,
and founded Transformation Project Prison Ministry
(TPPM), a 501(c)(3) non-profit corporation, in 2005.
TPPM produces MAXIMUM SAINTS books and DVDs
containing transformation stories of inmates at
ACDF. Chaplain McDonald founded GriefPathway
Ventures, LLC. in 2010 to help others learn how to
process grief and healing. In 2011, she founded the
Veterans Twofish Foundation, a 501(c)(3) non-profit
corporation, to provide emotional and educational
Support to veterans and veterans' families.

Resources

GriefPathway Ventures LLC

Yong Hui V. McDonald, also known as Vescinda McDonald, a United Methodist minister, founded GriefPathway Ventures LLC in 2010 to help others learn how to process grief and healing. They have published numerous books, DVDs, audiobooks and ebooks. You may purchase individual copies through Amazon.com.
Website: www.griefpathway.com
Email: greifpwv.gmail.com
Griefpathway Ventures LLC
P.O. Box 220, Brighton, CO 80601

Twisted Logic, The Shadow of Suicide is a how-to guide for dealing with people who are suffering with thoughts of suicide. This book will bring hope and understanding to the family that is walking in the grief of the painful reality of suicide.

Tornadoes, Grief, Loss, Trauma, and PTSD, Tornadoes, Lessons and Teachings—The TLT Model for Healing, "When we encounter crises or large problems in our lives, it truly does feel like being trapped in a tornado. With the rise of grief, loss, trauma, and PTSD over the past ten years, there is a true need for a way to heal spiritually. Chaplain McDonald accomplishes this by showing us how to use the TLT model, a simple tool that is easy to use and an effective way to process grief." — Cody Bushman

Veterans Twofish Foundation (VTF)

Veterans Twofish Foundation, a 501(c)(3)
nonprofit organization, produces, publishes,
and distributes stories of veterans and
veterans' families. They provide emotional and
spiritual support and encouragement to veterans and their
families through chaplains services. Your donation is 100%
tax deductible. If you would like to be a partner in this very
important mission of reaching out to veterans, or want to know
more about this project, please visit them online at: *www.
veteranstwofish.org, email: veteranstwofish@gmalil.com*
You may purchase individual copies through Amazon.com.
Veterans Twofish Foundation, P.O. Box 220, Brighton, CO 80601

In *Tornadoes of War, Inspirational Stories of
Veterans and Veteran's Families*, Yong Hui V.
McDonald speaks of a timely topic. There is
no greater respected group than our military
veterans. They have literally put their lives on
the line. The book offers interesting and
intriguing insights into the inner emotions
and experiences of this special group of
men and women.

In *Bitter Wind, A Memoir of War in Korea*,
Hui Chae Lee's personal journey reveals a
triumphant biography of a woman and her
family affected by war, as she battles its
aftermath of spiritual warfare with prayer and a
deep faith in Jesus Christ. Prepare to be
completely inspired by what God might do with
the powerful legacy this story offers to us.

In *Stand Strong, Spiritual Resiliency The
Ephesians Way*, Jack Scott Stanley provides a practical
study guide on Ephesians couched in the military terms
of spiritual combat. Well illustrated from the authors
personal experiences and examples from a wide range
of literature resources, the chapters end with reflective
questions. This book will appeal to a wide range of
audiences to include high school and college students
as well as adult study groups.

U.S. Department of Veterans Affairs (VA):

The VA provides a wide range of benefits including, Disability, Education and Training, Vocational Rehabilitation and Employment, Home Loan Guaranty, Dependant and Survivor Benefits, Medical Treatment, Life Insurance and Burial Benefits. For more information, go to: *www.va.gov*

Transformation Project Prison Ministry

The Transformation Project Prison Ministry (TPPM),a 501(c)(3) non-profit organization, produces, publishes books and DVDs and distributes them to prisons, jails, and homeless shelters nationwide. TPPM produces *Maximum Saints* books and DVDs containing transformation stories of inmates at Adams County Detention Facility, in Brighton, Colorado. You may purchase individual copies through Amazon.com.

Your donation is 100% tax deductible. TPPM has distributed over 100,000 books and DVDs free of charge. If you would like to be a partner in this very important mission of reaching out to prisoners and homeless, or want to know more about this project, please visit them online at: www.maximumsaint.org. You can donate on line or you can write a check addressed to:

Transformation Project Prison Ministry
5209 Montview Boulevard
Denver, CO 80207
Facebook: http://tinyurl.com/yhhcp5g

Book One: *Maximum Saints Never Hide in the Dark*
Book Two: *Maximum Saints Make No Little Plans*
Book Three: *Maximum Saints Dream*
Book Four: *Maximum Saints Forgive*
Book Five: *Maximum Saints All Things Are Possible*